THE SPIRALIZER COOKBOOK

70 + QUICK AND EASY RECIPES FOR DELICIOUS, SATISFYING MAIN DISHES, SOUPS, SALADS, SIDE DISHES AND MORE

JENNIFER WILLIAMS

PUBLISHERS NOTES

Table of Contents

Introduction

I love kitchen gadgets and accessories and virtually any new toy for the kitchen. So when I started seeing spiralizers, spiral slicers, spiral vegetable slicer, spiral cutters or whatever else you would like to call them, I was intrigued.

The concept of being able to get more vegetables into my diet and my daughter's diet is intriguing. If I could do that in a new and refreshing way, why not. The thought of just adding two to three more cups of broccoli to my daily diet is not at particularly appetizing. In fact it is incredibly difficult, at least for me. But, if I could add two more cups of vegetables by replacing the pasta in a dish or even making vegetables into more tasty side dishes and entrees was something I was definitely going to try.

All of the spiralizers and julienne peelers appeared to have a fun variety of spiral slices that you could make. Even a mandoline offered an array cuts that I could use in making my vegetable dishes. So with the goal of satisfying my intrigue with this latest gadget and with a goal of increasing my vegetables and reducing my carbohydrates, I was on a mission to find a spiral cutter. I wanted to find one that would work best for me and would help me add more vegetables to my daily diet.

There were so many options, but I found one that would work for me – more about that later – and I began to experiment. Most of the recipes I tried early on were designed to substitute the typical wheat pastas in a dish with zucchini noodles. They were very quick and easy to make and very delicious and satisfying.

I wondered if there were any more ways I could use my new found kitchen gadget. After all, we don't eat spaghetti or a pasta dish every day. Jazzing up a salad seemed obvious. I wanted to try new types of salads with a variety of ingredients. But what if I could take this idea to delicious and creative new main dishes and side dishes, or just update versions of the classic favorites with spiral vegetables.

What I soon realized was that there was so much more I could do with this handy little gadget. First I could test all kinds of vegetables and fruits in varying combinations. I could make servings for one to 12 and more if I wanted. I was very excited!

After trying many different variations for myself, some outstanding and some that were seriously questionable, I came up with numerous easy, inviting and delicious main dishes and side dishes, that I was ready to try on friends. Even better, it was a great excuse for dinner parties. Not only did we have fun get-togethers, but I was able to get valuable feedback for my recipes. I asked for honest evaluations so I could get the best sampling of recipes for this book.

The next true test was my going to be my college-age daughter; a valuable and brutally honest critic. Changing or updating some of her long time favorites was going to prove difficult, or so I thought. She was delighted with the dishes she tried and was also excited about eating healthier dishes.

This recipe book is a result of my recipe testing and the taste testing and wonderful feedback from many people on their favorite spiral veggie dishes.

My goal was to create new recipes for salads, soups, main dishes and sides that would be both healthier and more appealing to eat more vegetables.

I do include many updated classic and comfort food recipes. But I've also expanded the boundaries of flavorful vegetables that you can make at home quickly and easily too. There are indeed the recipes for vegetarians, gluten-free diets and low carbohydrate diets. But, there are also a wide variety of dishes for meat, poultry and fish lovers and salad or side dishes that will go with any meal. Expanding the boundaries of traditional vegetable dishes gives you so many more options that you will be able to serve in so many ways!

A spiral slicer can do wonders to your vegetables and fruits, however this recipe book takes it to the next level, and with it you will be able to quickly and easily add variety to your diet and please your family, friends, and yourself with delicious, beautiful looking dishes.

The best part? These recipes are tasty and nutritious and can be made quickly and easily! Happy spiralizing!

Acknowledgments

I cannot even begin to thank the many people that made this book possible without first and foremost giving my heartfelt thanks to my mother. Her endless love and encouragement taught me that you can accomplish anything. Without that, this book would not have been possible.. I wish you were here now to see this book come to life.

To my grandma Ida and grandpa John, who gave me the appreciation for a variety of vegetables and home cooked meals. I so enjoyed romping around their small farm when I was young. Every day we enjoyed a variety of fresh, delicious vegetables in many different dishes.

To my aunt and godmother Lorraine, who through her cooking and baking showed me that zucchini was not an 'icky' vegetable if you learned how to use it.

The support of my dear friend Karla Rabusch continues to keep me motivated and excited about my new cookbook ventures. On a recent visit to her home in San Francisco, the importance of eating lighter was reaffirmed when I was walking the hills of the city. The variety of delicious foods we ate and the experiences of the neighborhoods there inspired a number of recipes in this book.

Special thanks to my taste testers and my wonderful daughter Natalie for endlessly testing recipes and giving me your valuable feedback, support and encouragement.

Getting Started

If you are looking for a new twist on healthy cooking and more tantalizing ways to eat more vegetables and fruits, then spiralizing is for you. You can create delicious dishes that are not only quick and easy, but also sumptuous to look at.

Using a spiral vegetable cutter is a much faster way to cut vegetables and fruits into a variety of shapes for your soups, salads, main dishes and sides.

Long, appealing slices are perfect for a healthy alternative to traditional pasta. Their shapes are also ideal for stir fries, soups or salads and side dishes. Spiral vegetable cutters also make beautiful garnishes for appetizers and an endless array of dishes.

About Spiralizers, Spiral Slicers, Julienne Peelers, Mandolines and other Vegetable Cutters

Each of these tools is a small kitchen gadget that makes cutting vegetables and fruits into thin, long slices an extremely easy, streamlined process that takes a lot of time out of preparing vegetables and fruits for your dishes.

Spiralizers and Spiral Slicers: There are a vast number these gadgets in the market today. You can find them at Amazon, kitchen stores and big box retailers.

There are essentially three different types of spiralizers and within these, there are many brands and nuances among these types.

The **first type** is the largest. It features 3 to 4 different size cutting blades. You can cut anything from spaghetti size noodles, to fettuccine, to wider tagliatelle or egg noodle sized pasta. This picture is representative of the larger types of spiralizers.

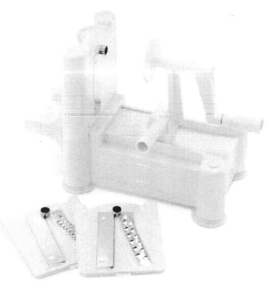

The advantages with this type are; the larger base with suction cups that hold to your cupboard; the hand crank keeps your fingers away from the blades and gives you more leverage for turning denser vegetables.

The disadvantages include the overall size of this gadget is bigger. If you have limited counter or storage space this is not a good choice. Some brands have a platform that extends beyond the blades while cutting while others do not. This is a nice feature to have since your spiral cut produce can drop directly into a bowl or other container that you are using. Thus the cleanup is less and you save a step in the preparation process. The blades are also exposed so caution is required when changing and cleaning blades.

The **second type** is a midsize kitchen tool. It typically features 4 different size cutting blades. It is much more compact that the previously mentioned type. This picture is representative of the medium size spiralizers.

This is the one that I use. There are a number of things that I like about this spiralizer. First, it takes up very little space both while I am working with it and when I am ready to store it away. There are 4 cutting sizes. I am able to change the cutting size simply by turning that little knob on the side of the tool; I don't have to manually change any blades.

I can also cut produce directly into any bowl or cooking pan that I am using. But, I can also cut my produce directly into the storage container that comes with it. This feature is really nice for cutting onions; I can cut them directly into the bowl, cover them, and store them for use at a later time.

Cleaning this gadget is also extremely easy and there are fewer parts to clean. Mine came with a small wire brush that makes cleaning the blades very easy.

The **third type** is a small, handheld kitchen tool. It features two blades for thin or thicker pasta strands. This picture is representative of the smaller size spiralizers.

It is ideally suited for making noodles out of vegetables or fruits. The blades will not give you a wider cut. But if you want to just make spaghetti sized noodles this is a good, compact tool for that purpose. The produce you are cutting fits into the cone shape and using one hand to hold the device, you turn the vegetable or fruit into the cutting blades. Clean up is relatively easy. However, you do need to be careful handling the device to avoid coming into contact with the sharp blades.

Julienne Peelers: These kitchen tools have been around for a long time. You can find them at just about anywhere you can buy small kitchen gadgets; Amazon, kitchen stores, big box retailers and even at your well stocked grocery store.

There are various cutting blades on different brands and types. Make sure you find on that has ultra-sharp, serrated blades and that the blade sizes are ideal for the size cuts you want to prepare. They are small and compact and can typically fit in most utensil drawers.

Mandolines: These kitchen tools have also been around for a long time and can also be purchased at just about anywhere you can buy small kitchen gadgets. I also use one of these in my kitchen, particularly if I want to make very wide cuts; this works very well for cutting eggplant into wide lasagna noodle size slices.

Look for mandolines that have multiple size cutting blades and a thickness adjuster that will give you various size cuts for the dishes you will be preparing. Also make sure your mandoline has a food holder that securely holds food and protects fingers. The one pictured above also has non-slip feet and a handle for securing your tool while cutting. You can also find mandolines that have claps to securely fit the tool over bowls or other containers.

Other Spiral Vegetable Cutters: If you have a food processor or a stand mixer with the ability to add attachments, you can also use these appliances to cut your vegetables and fruits. There are blades and attachments for slicing, julienne cuts, shredding and grinding. Your ability to make spiralized produce depends upon the brand of appliance you have and the attachments that are available for it.

While this is an option, it is harder if not impossible to get the long spiral cuts you would like for a spaghetti or fettuccine dish. The cleanup is also much more tedious with these types of appliances because of the many parts.

Other Handy Tools

Aside from whichever spiral vegetable cutter you choose, there are just a few other kitchen tools, besides the standard pots and pans, that you will need to make your spiralized dishes.

Large Sharp knife: To cut off the ends of your produce and to cut denser, harder vegetables, a large sharp knife is the best tool for the task. You can also use a knife to peel your vegetables if desired.

Vegetable peeler: Makes the task of peeling vegetables and fruits much easier.

Strainer: If you want to eliminate some of the moisture from your vegetables, particularly zucchini before you add them to your dishes a strainer works very well. You can also just drain your vegetables on paper towels.

Garlic Press: While this gadget isn't a necessity, you will find that mincing garlic is a snap with one of these tools instead of mincing with a knife.

The Spiralizing Pantry

The beauty of spiralizing your vegetables, particularly if you are substituting them for traditional wheat pasta is that you can eliminate gluten, reduce your calories and lower your intake of carbohydrates.

You will also be able to increase your daily recommended allowance of vegetables and fruits in a variety of delicious, satisfying dishes.

Vegetables and Fruits

Always use the best produce you can find. The quality of produce you put in to your cooking will most certainly determine the quality of your final dish. Why go through the time, money and energy if you are not striving for the best you can make. It takes the same amount of time to use either, but you will be happier with your end result.

Fully ripened vegetables and fruits should always be used. Not over-ripe and not under-ripe; either of these will produce inferior results. You will also get the best results by choosing produce that is in season in your area. Not only will the flavor and texture be better, but local in-season vegetables and fruits often cost less.

One the of most common and favorite vegetables, among people who love to spiralize, is zucchini. This is a very common substitute for conventional wheat pasta in recipes. However there are a wide variety of vegetables and fruits you can use with your spiral vegetable cutters to make delicious meals and sides. Some of the best vegetables to spiralize are: zucchini, winter and summer squash, sweet potatoes, russet potatoes, carrots, cucumbers, parsnips, turnips, beets, rutabaga, kohlrabi, eggplant, cabbage, radishes, onions and celery root (celeriac). Ideal fruits include apples, pears and jicama.

As a general rule of thumb, you will achieve the best results if you choose thick, firm and straight vegetables and fruits.

Herbs, Seasonings and Flavorings

When adding fresh or dried herbs, seasonings and flavorings remember that a little goes a long way. Always follow the recommended recipe amounts to make sure you get the correct flavor and consistency. If you are confident in your skills and experience with making these recipes, then you may want to adjust the amounts but do so only in small increments.

If you want to use dried herbs instead of fresh, as a general rule of thumb use 1/3 the amount of dried herbs as fresh. For example, if your recipe calls for 3 tbsp of fresh parsley, you could substitute 1 tbsp of dried. Keep in mind that dried herbs will have the same purity of flavor as fresh herbs.

Oils and Vinegars

A standard in many of these recipes is the use of olive oil or vegetable oil. Coconut oil or nut oils such as peanut or sunflower are also a good oils to have on hand.

Vinegar is a pantry staple. Vinegar is one of the most useful ingredients in your kitchen so you will want to make sure you have this item on hand. The acidity and sourness of vinegar is essential to how we taste and enjoy our foods. Vinegar can impact the texture, color, flavor and thickness of our foods.

There are dozens of types of vinegars each adding its own flavor and texture to your dish. If you are unsure which ones to have on hand, start with the basics when following a recipe and then expand your palate from there. Whatever you choose, make sure you have this prized ingredient in your pantry.

Broths and Condiments

Chicken, vegetable and beef broth are wonderful ingredients for simmering vegetable noodles. Broths add a deep flavor to soups and simmering meats. You can make your broth from scratch, buy containers or canned or use bouillon cubes.

Versatile condiments that will add zest and unique flavoring to your dishes include Dijon mustard, sriracha, Worcestershire sauce and honey. These are just a few of the items you will want to have on hand for your cooking. They can be used in many other dishes in arsenal.

Get Ready, Get Set

Scan the ingredient lists of the recipes that appeal to you to make sure you have everything you need for the dishes you want to prepare. When using fresh vegetables and fruits, you should purchase them just in time, or at the most within 2 to 3 days, to make your meals for best results.

You will have the most success with your dishes if you have all of the ingredients prepped ahead of time and have them ready to go. Many of the vegetables need very little cooking time, so having your other ingredients ready will help you avoid overcooking and getting soggy noodles.

Always add the ingredients in the order listed and according to the recipe directions.

Quick Tips for Best Results

Use the manual that is included with your spiralizer or spiral vegetable cutter on how to assemble it, if necessary, and the instructions for how to use it and how to get the best results. The manufacturer knows best how you should use their slicers.

Choose thick, firm and straight vegetables and fruits.

Pick vegetables that are not overly large since you will not be able to handle them as nimbly and they may not fit properly in your spiralizer.

Use vegetables that little or no seeds in them. If they do have seed, such as a cucumber, the thinner they are the fewer seeds they will have.

Always use fully ripe vegetables and fruits. Use the best quality you can find to yield superior results. Wash them and make sure they are dry before using.

Position your vegetables or fruit as straight as possible into the spiralizer.

Measure your ingredients carefully to get ideal results. When you are cooking vegetables, it is better to not have them overcrowded in their pan, pot or bowl.

Clean your gadget promptly after using. If you have a kitchen brush, or if one was included with your purchase, use that to clean your slicer right after use.

Safety Tips

As with any cutting tool, the blade edges are very sharp on any spiralizer, spiral slicer, julienne peeler, mandoline or other vegetable cutter. Take caution when cutting your produce and also when cleaning. After washing your cutters, dry the blades carefully to prevent rust or tarnishing.

Chapter 1
Salads and Soups

Kohlrabi Salad with Feta Cheese and Dried
Cranberries

Rainbow Salad

Kohlrabi, Radish and Asparagus Salad

Thai Salad with Peanut Lime Dressing

Greek Cucumber Salad

Curry Zucchini Pasta Salad with Tomatoes and Mango

Zucchini Noodle Salad with Corn and Tomatoes

Korean Sweet Potato Salad

Caprese Zucchini Salad

Sweet and Sour Cucumber Noodles

Spinach and Apple Salad with Pecans, Cranberries
and Feta

Cucumber Noodles with Spicy Sesame Soy Dressing

Curried Chickpea and Veggie Salad

Beet, Radish and Apple Slaw

Crispy Sweet Potato, Spinach and Walnut Salad

Kohlrabi Salad with Feta Cheese and Dried Cranberries

This delightful combination of vegetables, cheese, cranberries and nuts pleases on so many levels.

PREP TIME:

15 Minutes

TOTAL TIME:

15 Minutes

SERVES:

1

INGREDIENTS

1 – 1 1/2 cups baby arugula

1 kohlrabi, peeled and spiralized

1 green apple, spiralized

1/4 cup crumbled feta cheese

2 tbsp chopped walnuts, toasted

1 tbsp dried cranberries

1 1/2 – 2 tbsp salad dressing

DIRECTIONS

1. Place the arugula in a bowl. 2. Using a spiralizer or julienne peeler, spiralize kohlrabi and green apples into

spaghetti size strands. Add kohlrabi and green apple strands on top of arugula.

2. Add feta cheese, dried cranberries and walnuts.

3. Add salad dressing to taste.

COOK'S NOTE: Add your favorite salad dressing or make the Classic Vinaigrette in Chapter 4.

Rainbow Salad

Color, crunch and a burst of flavor are the defining characteristics of this refreshing salad.

PREP TIME:

30 Minutes

TOTAL TIME:

30 Minutes

SERVES:

2

INGREDIENTS

2 English cucumbers, spiralized

2 large carrots, spiralized

1 large beet, spiralized

1 mango, julienned

2 tbsps salad dressing

DIRECTIONS

1. Using a spiralizer or julienne peeler, spiralize cucumbers, carrots and beet into long spaghetti size noodles. Cut with kitchen shears into shorter strands, if desired. Toss vegetable strands with mango and dressing until well coated.

COOK'S NOTES: You can use a regular cucumber and remove the seeds before spiralizing.

Add your favorite salad dressing or make the Basil-Garlic Dressing recipe in Chapter 4.

Kohlrabi, Radish and Asparagus Salad

A crunchy salad that is great for a side dish or a light and refreshing mid-day meal.

PREP TIME:

10 Minutes

STANDING TIME:

30 Minutes to 1 hour

TOTAL TIME:

40 Minutes

SERVES:

2

INGREDIENTS

1 large kohlrabi peeled, spiralized

2 large red radishes, spiralized

3 thick asparagus stalks shaved (using a julienne peeler)

1 tbsp sunflower seeds, roasted and salted

2 tbsps salad dressing

DIRECTIONS

1. Using a spiralizer or julienne peeler, spiralize the kohlrabi into fettuccini size noodles. Spiralize the radishes into spaghetti size noodles. Shave asparagus

into 3 to 4 in lengths. Add kohlrabi, radishes, and asparagus together into a bowl.

2. Pour dressing over the noodles and toss to combine. Let stand for 30 min to 1 hr for flavors to meld properly. Transfer to a serving bowl and sprinkle with sunflower seeds.

COOK'S NOTES:

Add your favorite salad dressing or make the Lemon-Chive Dressing recipe in Chapter 4.

Thai Salad with Peanut Lime Dressing

A bounty of vegetables is topped by a sassy peanut lime dressing that will awaken your tasted buds.

PREP TIME:

30 Minutes

COOK TIME:

0 Minutes

TOTAL TIME:

30 Minutes

SERVES:

2

INGREDIENTS

1 cup Napa cabbage, chopped

1/3 cup jicama, spiralized

2/3 cup carrots, spiralized

2/3 cup yellow beets, spiralized

4 tbsp Peanut Lime Dressing (recipe in Chapter 4)

3 slices cucumber, halved

2 tsp chopped unsalted peanuts

1 lime wedge

2 - 3 tbsp chopped fresh cilantro

DIRECTIONS

1. Put Napa cabbage in a large, shallow serving bowl.

2. Using a spiralizer or julienne peeler, spiralize the jicama, carrots and yellow beets into spaghetti size noodles.

3. Add spiralized vegetables to top of cabbage in bowl. Drizzle with 2 to 4 tbsp Peanut Lime Dressing, or to taste.

3. Garnish with the cucumber, peanuts, lime, and cilantro.

COOK' NOTES:

The Peanut Lime Dressing can be stored in your refrigerator for up to 1 week.

Use any remaining dressing on a variety of salads or use as dipping sauce for chicken drummies.

Alternatively, you can use a store-bought Peanut dressing instead of making your own.

Greek Cucumber Salad

The Mediterranean comes to life with the refreshing tastes of the delightful salad. Serve as a main dish or as a side – either way you are sure to enjoy it.

PREP TIME:

15Minutes

COOK TIME:

0 Minutes

TOTAL TIME:

15 Minutes

SERVES:

1

INGREDIENTS

1 English cucumber, or 1 standard cucumber, seeded

1/4 green bell pepper, chopped

1/3 cup cherry tomatoes, cut in half

5 kalamata olives, pitted

1 tbsp red onion, thinly sliced

1/2 fresh lemon

1 oz feta, thickly sliced

1/2 tbsp olive oil

1 tsp fresh oregano leaves, minced

Kosher salt

Freshly ground black pepper

DIRECTIONS

1. Cut the cucumber into (approximately) 5 inch lengths. Using a spiralizer or julienne peeler, spiralize the cucumber into fettuccine size noodles.

2. Place the cucumber spirals in a large bowl. Add the bell pepper, tomatoes, olives and red onion. Squeeze 1/2 of the juice from the lemon over the top. Drizzle with half of the olive oil. Add the oregano. Add salt and pepper to taste. Toss gently until even coated.

3. Place salad on a serving plate. Top with a slice of feta. Drizzle with remaining olive oil.

COOK'S NOTE: This recipe can easily be expanded for as many servings as you would like.

Curry Zucchini Pasta Salad with Tomatoes and Mango

A delightful salad with a touch of both spicy curry and cooling vegetables and fruits.

PREP TIME:

10 Minutes

COOK TIME:

0 Minutes

TOTAL TIME:

10 Minutes

SERVES:

1

INGREDIENTS

1 medium zucchini, spiralized

2 tsp olive oil

Sea salt

1 tbsp chopped basil

1 – 2 tsp curry powder

2 cups baby salad greens

4 cherry tomatoes, cut in half

1/2 mango, cut into large cubes

Fresh parsley or cilantro, (optional)

DIRECTIONS

1. Using a spiralizer or julienne peeler, spiralize the zucchini into spaghetti size noodles into a small bowl.

2. Add olive oil, sea salt and basil to zucchini. Add curry powder, to the level of spice you prefer. Toss gently to coat. Set aside.

3. On a salad plate, add salad greens, tomatoes and mango. Top with zucchini mixture. Add fresh parsley, if using.

Zucchini Noodle Salad with Corn and Tomatoes

A zesty champagne vinaigrette marinates the zucchini noodles in this refreshing salad.

PREP TIME:

5 Minutes

TOTAL TIME:

5 Minutes

SERVES:

4

INGREDIENTS

4 medium zucchini, spiralized

1 1/2 cups fresh corn kernels, about 2 cobs

1 pint cherry tomatoes, halved

1/4 cup champagne vinegar

1/4 cup olive oil

1/4 cup sesame seed oil

1 garlic clove, minced

1/2 tsp Kosher salt

1/4 tsp granulated sugar

3 tbsp loosely chopped basil leaves, (optional)

1/2 cup shaved Parmesan cheese

DIRECTIONS

1. Using a spiralizer or julienne peeler, spiralize zucchini into spaghetti size noodles.

2. In a pasta serving bowl, combine the zucchini, corn, and tomatoes.

2. In a 1 to 2 cup tightly sealed container, combine the vinegar, oils, garlic, salt, and sugar. Shake vigorously to combine.

3. Pour the vinaigrette over the salad, and toss to coat. Let stand for 5 to 10 minutes, or until noodles have softened and vinaigrette worked into ingredients. Sprinkle basil leaves, if using, and Parmesan cheese on top of salad.

Korean Sweet Potato Salad

This salad is similar to the traditional Japchae dish but instead of the usual noodles made with sweet potato starch, this recipe uses fresh sweet potatoes.

PREP TIME:

10 Minutes

COOK TIME:

20 Minutes

TOTAL TIME:

30 Minutes

SERVES:

4

INGREDIENTS

2 large sweet potatoes, peeled and spiralized

3 carrots, spiralized

3 1/3 tbsp sesame oil, divided

1/4 cup soy sauce, or tamari (for gluten-free)

1 tbsp maple syrup

1 yellow onion, thinly sliced

4 oz baby portabella mushrooms, sliced

1 red bell pepper, thinly sliced

6-8 stems of kale, remove stems and chop

2 tbsp toasted sesame seeds

6 - 8 green onions, finely sliced

DIRECTIONS

1. Using a spiralizer or julienne peeler, spiralize the sweet potatoes into spaghetti size noodles.

2. Spiralized the carrots, cut into 4 inch lengths and set aside.

3. In a large deep skillet, toss sweet potato noodles with 2 tsp sesame oil and cook over medium-low heat, until slightly softened. Remove from heat.

4. In a small bowl, combine soy sauce, 2 tbsp sesame oil and maple syrup. Blend well. Add to sweet potatoes in pan and gently toss. Add mixture to serving plate.

5. In another pan, sauté onion with 2 tsp sesame oil, until transparent. Add mushrooms, carrots, red pepper and kale. Toss until greens are heated through and slightly soft. Add to top of sweet potatoes.

6. Sprinkle with sesame seeds and green onions.

Caprese Zucchini Salad

This refreshing and colorful salad, named after the Island of Capri, is a delicious side salad. Or, skewer the ingredients for a festive appetizer presentation with the colors of the Italian flag.

PREP TIME:

10 Minutes

COOK TIME:

0 Minutes

TOTAL TIME:

10 Minutes

SERVES:

4

INGREDIENTS

3 medium zucchini, spiralized

1 cup cherry tomatoes, halved

1/2 lb. fresh bocconcini

1 tbsp olive oil

2 tsp balsamic vinaigrette

1/2 tsp red pepper flakes

1/4 cup basil, chiffonade or chopped

Sea salt (optional)

Fresh ground black pepper (optional)

DIRECTIONS

1. Using a spiralizer or julienne peeler, spiralize the zucchini into spaghetti size noodles.

2. Add tomatoes and bocconcini. Drizzle with olive oil and balsamic vinaigrette. Sprinkle with basil, red pepper flakes and salt and pepper, if using.

Sweet and Sour Cucumber Noodles

One of my favorite dishes was when my mother made cucumber salad. She always had to cut more cucumbers than needed for the recipe, because I would always snitch more ahead of time because they are just so good.

PREP TIME:

5 Minutes

TOTAL TIME:

5 Minutes

SERVES:

4

INGREDIENTS

3 medium cucumbers, spiralized

1/2 small red onion, sliced and quartered

3/4 cup rice vinegar

2 1/2 tsp sugar

1 1/2 tsp white sesame seeds

DIRECTIONS

1. Using a spiralizer or julienne peeler, spiralize the cucumber into wide noodles, similar to Tagliatelle or

egg noodles, directly into a bowl.

2. Add the red onion, rice vinegar, sugar and 1/4 cup water. Cover the bowl tightly and refrigerate the cucumber noodles for a minimum of 2 hours, stirring occasionally, until flavors meld and salad is well chilled.

3. Top with sesame seeds and serve.

Spinach and Apple Salad with Pecans, Cranberries and Feta

A spinach salad takes a new twist with spiral cut apples and flavorful toppings for an elegant salad that can be made in minutes.

PREP TIME:

5 Minutes

COOK TIME:

0 Minutes

TOTAL TIME:

5 Minutes

SERVES:

4

INGREDIENTS

2 tbsp extra virgin olive oil

1 tbsp Dijon mustard

2 tbsp balsamic vinegar

1 tbsp honey

Salt (optional)

Ground black pepper (optional)

4 Fuji apples (or similar), spiralized

6 cups baby spinach

1/2 cup pecans

1/3 cup dried cranberries

1/3 cup feta cheese

DIRECTIONS

1. Put olive oil, Dijon mustard, balsamic vinegar and honey into a bowl. Add salt and pepper if using. Whisk ingredients together until combined. Set aside.

2. Using a spiralizer or julienne peeler, spiralize the apples into spaghetti size noodles.

3. Add spinach, apples and dressing to serving bowl. Add dressing and toss to combine. Sprinkle with pecans, cranberries and feta cheese. Serve.

Cucumber Noodles with Spicy Sesame Soy Dressing

A crispy, cool and spicy salad that is satisfying as a meal or served as a side dish.

PREP TIME:

20 Minutes

COOK TIME:

0 Minutes

TOTAL TIME:

20 Minutes

SERVES:

6

INGREDIENTS

4 medium cucumbers, spiralized

2 large carrots, spiralized

1 garlic clove, minced

1 tbsp lime juice

1/2 tbsp rice wine vinegar

1/4 cup soy sauce

1 tbsp sesame oil

1 tsp fresh grated ginger

1 tsp honey

1 to 2 tsp sriracha

Pinch red pepper flakes

Cilantro for garnish (optional)

DIRECTIONS

1. Using a spiralizer or julienne peeler, spiralize the zucchini and carrots into spaghetti size noodles. Place the noodles in a bowl.

2. In a mixing bowl, whisk together the garlic, lime juice, vinegar, soy sauce, sesame oil, ginger and honey. Add 1 to 2 tsp sriracha sauce, or as much as you would like for your preferred spice level.

3. Add the dressing and the red pepper flakes to the noodles. Toss gently to coat noodles. Garnish with cilantro, if using.

Curried Chickpea and Veggie Salad

This Indian inspired salad is light, delicious and vegan and gluten-free.

PREP TIME:

10 Minutes

COOK TIME:

0 Minutes

TOTAL TIME:

10 Minutes

SERVES:

2 to 3

INGREDIENTS

2 carrots, spiralized

2 medium zucchini, spiralized

1 cup green cabbage cut into thin strips

1 red bell pepper, seeds removed, cut into thin strips

3 green onions, sliced

1/4 cup fresh cilantro, chopped

1 can chickpeas, drained and rinsed

Pinch salt (optional)

Pinch pepper (optional)

Pinch red chili flakes (optional)

1/3 cup tahini

2 tbsp lime juice

3 tbsp maple syrup

1 tbsp curry powder

1 tsp ground ginger

DIRECTIONS

1. In a large bowl, add tahini, lime juice, maple syrup, curry powder and ground ginger. Mix well. Add water, if needed, to reach desired consistency.

2. Using a spiralizer or julienne peeler, spiralize the carrots and zucchini into spaghetti size noodles. In a large bowl, add noodles, cabbage, bell pepper, green onions, cilantro and chickpeas. Add dressing and toss well to coat.

3. Season with salt, pepper, and red chili flakes, if using.

Beet, Radish and Apple Slaw

A colorful, zesty slaw delivers a refreshing surprise as either a side salad or a wrap.

PREP TIME:

10 Minutes

COOK TIME:

10 Minutes

TOTAL TIME:

15 Minutes

SERVES:

3 to 4

INGREDIENTS

1 large red beet, spiralized

1 bunch (5 to 7) radishes, spiralized

1 tart, green apple, spiralized

1/4 cup rice vinegar

2 tsp soy sauce

1/3 cup chopped cilantro plus sprigs for garnish

2 tbsp slivered Thai basil leaves

1 1/2 tbsp minced pickled ginger

2 tsp finely grated orange zest

Pinch salt (optional)

Romaine lettuce leaves

DIRECTIONS

1. Using a spiralizer or julienne peeler, spiralize the beet, radishes and apple into spaghetti size noodles.

2. In a large bowl, add the beets, radishes, apples, rice vinegar, soy sauce, cilantro, basil, ginger and orange zest. Toss together. Add salt, if using. Let rest 3 to 5 minutes to meld flavors.

3. Line plates with lettuce leaves and top with the slaw.

Crispy Sweet Potato, Spinach and Walnut Salad

A delicate spinach salad takes the forefront with a zesty mustard vinaigrette topped with crispy sweet potatoes and toasted walnuts.

PREP TIME:

10 Minutes

COOK TIME:

15 Minutes

TOTAL TIME:

25 Minutes

SERVES:

4

INGREDIENTS

3 large sweet potatoes peeled

2 tbsp olive oil

Salt

1/2 cup walnuts, chopped

1 bunch baby spinach leaves

1/2 cup crumbled feta cheese

1/2 cup scallions, roughly chopped

3 tbsp extra virgin olive oil

2 tbsp sherry vinegar

1 tsp mustard

1 garlic clove, minced

DIRECTIONS

1. Preheat the oven to 425 degrees.

2. Using a spiralizer or julienne peeler, spiralize the sweet potatoes into spaghetti size noodles. Toss with 2 tbsp olive oil and salt. Place on a large roasting pan, covered with foil or parchment paper. Roast for 10 to 15 minutes, turning occasionally, until golden brown..

3. During the last 5 minutes of roasting, on a separate baking sheet, add the walnuts and toast in the oven, tossing once, until fragrant.

4. Place the spinach in a large bowl and add the feta cheese and scallions. Put the olive oil, vinegar, mustard and garlic in a jar and shake well. Pour over the spinach.

5. Scatter the warm sweet potato spirals and toasted walnuts over the top. Serve.

COOK'S NOTE:

Top this salad with cooked chicken strips for a superb and satisfying main dish.

Chapter 2
Main Dishes

Pancetta and Lentils with Zucchini Pasta

Creamy Alfredo Pasta with Prosciutto and Vegetables

Pancetta, Chèvre and Candied Walnut Sweet Potato Pasta

Pork Sugo with Rutabaga Noodles

Creamy Prosciutto and Peas with Spaghetti

Winter Squash Carbonara with Pancetta and Sage

Spinach and Italian Sausage Eggplant Zucchini Lasagna

Beef Bolognese with Zucchini

Pork and Zucchini Noodle Bowls

Curry Beef with Sweet Potato Noodles

Italian Potato Spaghetti Pie

Mexican Chayote Squash Spaghetti Pie

Chicken Tetrazzini

Apple Chicken Sausages with Rutabagas,
   Caramelized Red Onions and Radicchio

Chicken Paprikash

Garlic and Herb Lemon Chicken with Roasted
   Delicata Squash

Leftover Turkey Tetrazzini

Chicken and Tangy Peanut Sauce over Squash
   and Carrot Noodles

Chicken Zucchini Lasagna

Lemon-Garlic Chicken with Zucchini Noodles

Chicken Tostadas

Chicken, Sweet Potato and Brie Galette

Mediterranean Chicken With Artichoke Hearts
   and Olives

Savory Skillet Turkey Sausage with Potato-
   Celeriac Noodles

Tuna Noodle Casserole

Grilled Shrimp with Zucchini Noodles and
   Lemon Basil Dressing

Zucchini and Carrot Wrap with Feta and
  Avocado

Sweet Potato Noodle Bolognese

Zucchini Fettuccine with Creamy Butternut
  Rosemary Sauce

Lentil Marinara with Zucchini Spaghetti

Spaghetti with Butter-Roasted Tomato Sauce

Zucchini Fettuccine with Peas and Sage Sauce

Zucchini Fettuccine with Rosemary Butternut
  Cream Sauce

Roasted Sweet Potato, Butternut Squash and
  Asparagus Pasta

Spring Ramp Carbonara

Spinach and Eggplant Zucchini Lasagna

Beef and Pork Main Dishes

Pancetta and Lentils with Zucchini Pasta

Aromatic pancetta, onions and garlic in a lentil and tomato sauce provide rich flavor for the zucchini pasta.

PREP TIME:

5 Minutes

COOK TIME:

20 Minutes

TOTAL TIME:

25 Minutes

SERVES:

4

INGREDIENTS

6 medium zucchini, spiralized

2 tbsp olive oil

1/2 cup chopped pancetta

1/2 cup finely chopped onion

4 garlic cloves, minced

1/2 tsp red pepper flakes

1 - 14 -ounce can green (French) lentils, drained

1 - 28 -ounce can diced tomatoes, in juices

10 basil leaves, chiffonade or roughly chopped, divided

1 cup chicken broth (optional)

1/2 tsp salt

1/2 cup grated parmesan cheese, divided

Kosher salt (optional)

Fresh ground black pepper (optional)

DIRECTIONS

1. Using a spiralizer or julienne peeler, spiralize the zucchini into spaghetti size noodles. Pat dry. Set aside.

2. In a large skillet, heat olive oil over medium heat. Add the pancetta and sauté about 7 minutes, or until crispy. Add the onion sauté about 2 minutes, or until translucent. Next, add the garlic and red pepper flakes sauté about 2 minutes, or until garlic begins to brown.

3. Stir in the lentils, tomatoes, 8 chopped basil leaves and salt. Increase the heat to medium high and bring the sauce to a boil; cook 3 minutes. Add chicken broth, as needed, to thin the sauce, if desired. Reduce the heat to medium low and simmer, stirring occasionally, about 5 to 7 minutes, or until slightly thickened.

4. Add the zucchini to the sauce and cook 2 more minutes. Remove from heat. Add 1/4 cup parmesan. Season with salt and pepper, if using. Gently toss. Divide among serving dishes. Drizzle each with olive oil and top with the remaining parmesan and basil.

Creamy Alfredo Pasta with Prosciutto and Vegetables

Zucchini noodles give a lighter take on a creamy pasta Alfredo dish with a variety of tantalizing ingredients.

PREP TIME:

5 Minutes

COOK TIME:

10 Minutes

TOTAL TIME:

15 Minutes

SERVES:

4

INGREDIENTS

4 medium zucchini, spiralized

2 tbsp virgin olive oil

1 cup asparagus pieces

8 oz fresh mushrooms, sliced

2 oz. prosciutto, chopped

1/2 cup frozen peas, thawed

1/2 cup cherry tomatoes, cut in half

Alfredo Sauce, store bought

Pinch white pepper

Pinch ground nutmeg

Toasted pine nuts (optional)

Fresh basil (optional)

DIRECTIONS

1. Using a spiralizer or julienne peeler, spiralize the zucchini into spaghetti size noodles. Set aside.

2. In a medium frying pan, add the olive oil, asparagus, mushrooms and prosciutto. Sauté for 6 to 8 minutes, or until ingredients are softened and prosciutto is slightly crisp.

3. Add Alfredo sauce, peas and the zucchini to the sautéed ingredients. Toss gently and simmer on low heat for 2 to 3 minutes, or until sauce is heated through. Do not overheat as sauce may separate and curdle. Toss in the tomatoes and remove from heat.

4. Serve in pasta bowls and sprinkle with white pepper and nutmeg. Garnish toasted pine nuts and fresh basil, if using.

Pancetta, Chèvre and Candied Walnut Sweet Potato Pasta

The combination of ingredients in this delicious dish deliver a pleasant savory taste you are sure to enjoy.

PREP TIME:

10 Minutes

COOK TIME:

20 Minutes

TOTAL TIME:

30 Minutes

SERVES:

4

INGREDIENTS

1 cup walnuts, halves and pieces

1/4 cup granulated sugar

1 tbsp butter

2 large sweet potatoes, spiralized

1/2 tsp sea salt

1 cup diced pancetta

1 cup crumbled Chèvre

1/2 tbsp olive oil

2 tbsp water

DIRECTIONS

1. In a medium skillet, add walnuts, granulated sugar and butter. Heat over medium heat for 5 minutes, stirring constantly, or until all sugar is melted and nuts are coated. Remove from heat and transfer to a sheet of parchment paper and scparate the nuts immediately. Let stand for 5 to 7 minutes, or until coating hardens.

2. Using a spiralizer or julienne peeler, spiralize the sweet potatoes into spaghetti size noodles.

3. In a large sauté pan, heat olive oil over medium heat. Add sweet potato noodles and salt. Sauté for 6 to 8 minutes, or until noodles are softened. Remove noodles from pan and sct aside.

4 In the same pan, sauté pancetta over medium heat for 3 to 4 minutes, or until done to your liking.

5. Reduce heat to medium-low. Add 1/2 cup Chèvre and water, blend ingredients until cheese is just melted. Add sweet potato noodles to pan and toss to combine. Remove from heat.

6. Top with remaining 1/2 cup Chèvre and candied walnuts. Serve warm.

Pork Sugo with Rutabaga Noodles

This make ahead dish abounds with flavor. The sauce has a robust flavor, the meat hearty and tender and the rutabaga sweet and savory.

PREP TIME:

20 Minutes + overnight in the refrigerator

COOK TIME:

120 Minutes

TOTAL TIME:

140 Minutes

SERVES:

8 to 10

INGREDIENTS

3 lb pork shoulder

Kosher salt

Black pepper

1/2 cup canola oil

3 cups sliced yellow onion

1 cup carrots, sliced on a bias

1 cup celery, sliced on a bias

3 cloves garlic, minced

2 sprigs fresh rosemary leaves

5 fresh sage leaves

2tbsp tomato paste

1 cup dry white wine

8 cups chicken stock

3 tbsp butter

1 tsp chopped fresh parsley

Pinch chile flakes (optional)

Parmigiano-Reggiano, grated

5 medium rutabaga

DIRECTIONS

1. Preheat oven to 325.

2. Cut the pork shoulder into 4 sections. Season the pork shoulder with salt and pepper. Heat the oil in a Dutch oven and add the pork. Brown well on all sides, remove the pork, and set aside.

3. To the pot add the onions, carrot, celery, garlic, rosemary and sage. Sauté 5 to 7 minutes, or until onions are translucent. Add the tomato paste and cook over medium heat, stirring for 2 minutes. Deglaze the pan with the wine and cook until liquid is reduced by half..

4. Return the seared pork to the pot. Add chicken stock and bring to a simmer. Cover pot and cook in over for 2

hours, or until meat is tender. Remove from oven, allow to cool and refrigerate overnight.

5. When ready to serve, remove sugo from the refrigerator and discard any congealed fat. Over low heat, warm the sugo through. Remove the pork from the liquid. Pull the shoulder apart by hand, discard the fat and break the meat into large chunks.

6. Using a handheld or immersion blender, puree the liquid along with all of the vegetables and herbs. Bring to a simmer and reduce until it thickens and has a good body. Add the meat to the pot, bring to a boil and turn off heat.

7. Using a spiralizer or julienne peeler, spiralize the rutabaga into wide tagliatelle size noodles.

8. Warm half of the pork sugo in a pan with the butter, chopped parsley and chile flake, if using. Add half the rutabaga noodles to the pot. Cook the rutabaga noodles in the sugo for 5 to 7 minutes, or until rutabaga is al dente. Stir in some grated Parmigiano-Reggiano. Remove from heat and serve immediately, Serve with more Parmigiano to grate over the top of the pasta. Repeat for second half of sugo and noodles.

COOK'S NOTES:

If you want to reserve some of the pork sugo to serve another day, wait to spiralize the rutabaga until you are ready to make the dish. This dish is finished in two batches in order to blend the flavors more readily and not break the noodles.

Creamy Prosciutto and Peas with Spaghetti

A classic favorite that gets a makeover with butternut squash noodles.

PREP TIME:

3 Minutes

COOK TIME:

5 Minutes

TOTAL TIME:

8 Minutes

SERVES:

4

INGREDIENTS

1 10 ounce package frozen peas

4 zucchini, spiralized

4 tbsp butter

1/2 lb prosciutto thinly sliced, rolled up and cut into 1/4-inch-wide strips

2/3 cup heavy cream

Salt

Pinch freshly ground black pepper

1/2 - 3/4 cup grated Parmesan cheese

DIRECTIONS

1. Cook peas according to package directions. Set aside.

2. Bring a salted pot of water to a boil. Using a spiralizer or julienne peeler, spiralize the zucchini into spaghetti size noodles. Add the zucchini to the boiling water and cook for 2 to 3 minutes until noodles are al dente.

3. Drain noodles, return to pot and toss with butter. Add peas, prosciutto and cream. Toss to mix well and to separate prosciutto strips.

4. Season with salt and pepper.

5. Add Parmesan, according to your liking, and toss again. Serve immediately.

Winter Squash Carbonara with Pancetta and Sage

Butternut squash with a creamy sauce and then topped with pancetta imbues this dish with comfort food goodness.

PREP TIME:

5 Minutes

COOK TIME:

28 Minutes

TOTAL TIME:

33 Minutes

SERVES:

4

INGREDIENTS

2 tbsp olive oil

4 oz pancetta, chopped

1 tbsp fresh sage, finely chopped

1 small onion, chopped

2 garlic cloves, minced

Kosher salt

Freshly ground black pepper

1/2 cups chicken broth

1/2 cup heavy cream

1 butternut squash, spiralized

1/4 cup finely grated Pecorino (1 oz)

1 1/2 oz Pecorino, shaved

DIRECTIONS

1. Heat oil in a large skillet over medium-high heat. Add pancetta, reduce heat to medium, and sauté 8 to 10 minutes, or until crisp. Add sage and toss to coat. Using a slotted spoon, transfer pancetta and sage to a small bowl; set aside.

2. Add onion and garlic to skillet. Season with salt and pepper. Sauté, stirring occasionally, until onion is translucent. Approximately 6 to 8 minutes. Add broth and heavy cream. Bring to a soft boil.

3. Using a spiralizer or julienne peeler, spiralize the butternut squash into spaghetti size noodles. Add noodles to the skillet. Reduce heat and simmer noodles for 7 to 9 minutes, or until soft.

4. Mix in 1/4 cup Pecorino. Remove from heat.

5. Top with reserved pancetta and sage and shaved Pecorino. Serve immediately.

Spinach and Italian Sausage Eggplant Zucchini Lasagna

Great as a make ahead dish, this heavenly lasagna will is loaded with fresh vegetables, Italian sausage and cheese.

PREP TIME:

15 Minutes

COOK TIME:

70 Minutes

TOTAL TIME:

85 Minutes

SERVES:

8 - 10

INGREDIENTS

Cooking spray

2 medium zucchini, cut lengthwise into 6 slices

2 medium eggplant, peeled and cut lengthwise into 8 slices

1/4 cup + 4 tbsp olive oil, divided

Salt

Ground black pepper

12 oz fresh Italian mild ground sausage

1 medium onion, chopped

2 cloves garlic, minced

1 26 oz. jar chunky pasta sauce

1 teaspoon dried Italian seasoning

1/4 cup chopped fresh basil leaves, divided

1 15 oz. container ricotta cheese

1/2 cup grated Parmesan cheese

1 large egg, lightly beaten

2 cups shredded mozzarella cheese

1 5 oz. package cheese and garlic croutons, crushed

DIRECTIONS

1. Heat oven to 425°F. Coat two 15 x 10 x 1-inch baking pans with cooking spray. Cut the zucchini an eggplant using a mandoline for even slices. Arrange the zucchini and eggplant on baking sheets. Brush tops with 1/4 cup olive oil. Season with salt and pepper. Bake 12 to 15 minutes or until fork tender. Remove from oven. Reduce oven temperature to 375°F.

2. In a large skillet heat 1 tbsp olive oil over medium heat, add ground sausage and cook 7 to 8 minutes breaking

up into small pieces, until browned. Add onion and garlic and cook 3 to 5 minutes, or until onion is tender.

Stir in pasta sauce, Italian seasoning and 3 tablespoons basil. Remove from heat.

3. In a medium bowl, mix ricotta cheese, parmesan cheese and egg until blended.

4. Coat a 13 x 9 inch baking dish with cooking spray. Layer half of eggplant in baking dish. Top with half of ricotta cheese mixture, half of zucchini, 1 1/2 cups pasta sauce mixture and 1 cup mozzarella cheese. Top with remaining eggplant, ricotta mixture, zucchini and pasta sauce mixture.

5.Bake for 30 to 35 minutes or until hot and bubbly. Remove from oven.

6. In a small bowl, Combine crushed croutons and remaining 2 tablespoons olive oil. Toss to coat. Stir in remaining 1 cup mozzarella cheese. Sprinkle evenly over top. Bake an additional 5 to 10 minutes, until cheese is melted and croutons are lightly toasted. Remove from oven; let stand 10 minutes before cutting and serving. Sprinkle with remaining 1 tablespoon basil and serve.

COOK'S NOTES:

Use a mandoline to cut the eggplant and zucchini into even strips. Your task will be easier and the slices will cook evenly.

This is a wonderful make ahead dish. The lasagna can be cut into individual servings and refrigerated for up to 5 days or frozen up to 2 months.

You can eliminate the Italian sausage for a vegetarian version of this dish.

Beef Bolognese with Zucchini

An easy hearty dish that will please everyone and won't leave you feeling overstuffed like traditional pasta.

PREP TIME:

5 Minutes

COOK TIME:

45 Minutes

TOTAL TIME:

50 Minutes

SERVES:

4

INGREDIENTS

2 tbsp olive oil, divided

1 lb ground beef

1 yellow onion, chopped

4 garlic cloves, minced

2 28 oz cans crushed tomatoes

1/4 cup tomato paste

1 tsp dried basil

1/2 tsp dried thyme

1 tsp dried oregano

Salt (optional)

Ground black pepper (optional)

6 medium zucchini, spiralized

1/3 cup grated parmesan (optional)

DIRECTIONS

1. In a large saucepan, sauté ground beef over medium-high heat for 8 to 10 minutes, or until browned, breaking up the large chunks of meat as they cook. Drain fat from meat.

2. Add 1 tbsp olive oil and onions to the saucepan and sauté 5 to 7 minutes, or until onions are translucent.

3. To the meat mixture, add the garlic, tomatoes, tomato paste, basil, thyme, and oregano. Bring to a boil. Reduce heat, and simmer, covered, for 45 minutes to 55 minutes, stirring occasionally, until mixture is thickened. Season with salt and pepper, if using.

4. While sauce is simmering, using a spiralizer or julienne peeler, spiralize the zucchini into spaghetti size noodles. In a separate frying pan, add the remaining tablespoon of olive oil and sauté the zucchini pasta for 5 to 7 minutes, until desired tenderness is achieved.

5. Divide the pasta among serving plates and top with Bolognese. Sprinkle with parmesan, if using. Serve immediately.

Pork Zucchini Noodle Bowls

A robust Asian inspired dish that is reminiscent of your favorite spring roll but without rolling the rice paper.

PREP TIME:

3 Minutes

COOK TIME:

19 Minutes

TOTAL TIME:

21 Minutes

SERVES:

4

INGREDIENTS

1 tbsp peanut oil or olive oil

1 lb ground pork

1 small onion, diced

1 red bell pepper, diced

2 garlic cloves, minced

1/4 tbsp red pepper flakes

Pinch salt

Pinch pepper

3 medium zucchinis, spiralized

1 large carrot, spiralized

1 14 oz can coconut milk

1/2 cup cashew butter (or alternative)

1/4 cup gluten free soy sauce

3 tablespoons sriracha

2 tbsp lime juice

2 tbsp chopped fresh cilantro

2/3 cup bean sprouts (optional)

DIRECTIONS

1. Using a spiralizer or julienne peeler, spiralize the
   zucchini and carrots into spaghetti size noodles. Set
   aside on paper towel.

2. In a large skillet over medium heat, add oil, pork, onion,
   bell pepper, garlic, red pepper flakes, salt and pepper.
   Sauté 7 to 9 minutes, breaking up pork into small pieces,
   until pork is no longer pink and onions and peppers are
   softened. Toss in carrots and cook for 3 minutes. Toss in
   zucchini and cook for 2 to 3 minutes more, until carrots
   and zucchini are softened. Remove from heat and place
   in individual serving bowls.

3. Meanwhile, in a small saucepan over medium heat, whisk together coconut milk, butter, soy sauce, sriracha and lime juice. Reduce heat to low and cook for about 5 to 7 minutes, or until sauce is thickened to your desired consistency. Pour sauce over pork and vegetables in bowls. Toss to combine. Sprinkle with chopped cilantro. Top with bean sprouts, if using.

Curry Beef with Sweet Potato Noodles

An easy spicy beef curry that highlights the tender, velvety sweet potato noodles.

PREP TIME:

5 Minutes

COOK TIME:

145 Minutes (25 minutes active)

TOTAL TIME:

150 Minutes

SERVES:

4

INGREDIENTS

2 - 3 tbsp vegetable oil

1 lb beef stew meat, cut into 1-inch pieces

Pinch salt

Pinch ground black pepper

1 large onions, sliced

3 whole cloves

2 garlic clove, chopped

1 cinnamon stick

1 bay leaf

1/4 tsp dried crushed red pepper

3/4 cups whole milk

2 medium tomatoes, quartered

3 tablespoons Major Grey chutney

1 1/2 tbsp fresh lemon juice

1 tbsp minced ginger

1 tbsp curry powder

1/4 tsp salt

2 yellow squash, spiralized

2 zucchini, spiralized

3 tbsp chopped fresh cilantro

DIRECTIONS

1. In a large heavy skillet over medium-high heat, heat 1 tbsp oil. Add beef cubes, in batches for easier browning, and season with salt and pepper. Sear beef 7 minutes per batch, or until brown beef on all sides. Add oil if necessary between batches. Using slotted spoon, transfer to plate.

2. Heat remaining 1 tbsp oil in same skillet over medium heat. Add onions and sauté 5 to 7 minutes, until tender and brown. Return beef to pot. Add cloves, garlic,

cinnamon stick, bay leaf and red pepper. Stir 1 minute. Mix in milk, tomatoes, lemon juice, ginger, curry powder and 1/2 teaspoon salt and bring to boil. Reduce heat, cover and simmer, stirring occasionally, approximately 2 hours, or until beef is tender.

3. Remove cover and increase heat to medium. Continue cooking 5 to 7 minutes more, or until juices are slightly thickened.

4. Meanwhile, using a spiralizer or julienne peeler, spiralize the zucchini and yellow squash into spaghetti size noodles. Add noodles to beef curry mixture, toss gently, and cook 2 to 3 minutes more, or until noodles are softened to your liking. Top with cilantro and serve immediately.

Italian Potato Spaghetti Pie

This hearty potato noodle casserole is a quick and easy all-in-one meal that will keep everyone satisfied.

PREP TIME:

7 Minutes

COOK TIME:

35 Minutes

TOTAL TIME:

42 Minutes

SERVES:

6

INGREDIENTS

1 large sweet potato, spiralized

2 medium russet potatoes, spiralized

Nonstick cooking spray

1 tbsp butter, melted

1 egg, beaten

1/4 cup grated Parmesan

Cooking spray

2 tsp vegetable oil

8 oz ground Italian sausage

1/2 cup chopped onion

1/2 cup chopped green bell pepper

1 clove garlic, minced

1 8 oz can tomato sauce

1 tsp dried oregano

1 cup cottage cheese, drained

1/2 cup shredded mozzarella cheese

DIRECTIONS

1. Preheat oven to 350°F.

2. Using a spiralizer or julienne peeler, spiralize the potatoes into spaghetti size noodles. Stir in butter, egg and Parmesan.

3. Coat a 9-inch pie plate with cooking spray. Press potato mixture onto bottom and up sides of pie plate to form a crust.

4. In a medium skillet, heat oil over medium heat. Add ground sausage, onion, bell pepper, and garlic and cook 5 to 7 minutes, or until meat is brown and onion is tender. Drain. Stir in tomato sauce and oregano; heat through.

5. Spread cottage cheese evenly over the bottom and sides of the potato pie crust. Spread meat mixture over cottage cheese. Sprinkle with shredded mozzarella cheese.

6. Bake for 20 to 25 minutes, or until bubbly and heated through. Let cool 5 minutes. Cut into pie shaped wedges and serve.

Mexican Chayote Squash Spaghetti Pie

Tender chayote squash spaghetti forms a crust that's filled with beef picante sauce, green chiles, black olives and lots of cheese.

PREP TIME:

10 Minutes

COOK TIME:

50 Minutes

TOTAL TIME:

60 Minutes

SERVES:

6

INGREDIENTS

1 pound ground beef

2 cups picante sauce

1 4 1/2 oz can chopped green chiles

2 tsp olive oil

4 chayote squash, spiralized

2 tsp cumin

1/3 cup grated Parmesan cheese

1 egg beaten

1 tbsp butter, melted

1 cup ricotta cheese

1 cup shredded mozzarella cheese

DIRECTIONS

1. Preheat oven to 350°F.

2. In a medium skillet over medium-high heat, cook beef 7
   to 9 minutes, until meat is browned, breaking the meat
   into small chunks during cooking. Drain the fat. Add the
   picante sauce and green chiles to the skillet and cook 4
   to 6 minutes, or until hot and bubbling.

3. Using a spiralizer or julienne peeler, spiralize the
   chayote squash into spaghetti size noodles. In a large
   skillet, heat olive oil, add squash and sauté for 3 to 5
   minutes, or until squash is tender. Remove from pan and
   place in a medium bowl.

4. To the squash, add parmesan cheese, egg and butter. Mix
   well. Spread the mixture on the bottom and up the side
   of greased 10-inch pie plate. Spread the ricotta cheese in
   the spaghetti shell. Top with the beef mixture.

5. Bake for 30 minutes, or until hot and bubbling. Sprinkle
   with the mozzarella cheese. Let stand for 5 minutes. Cut
   into 6 wedges for serving.

Poultry Main Dishes

Chicken Tetrazzini

This dish has been a favorite of mine since childhood and continues to be a favorite for my daughter and me. I love that I can now make it with fewer carbohydrates and calories.

PREP TIME:

30 Minutes

COOK TIME:

30 Minutes

TOTAL TIME:

60 Minutes

SERVES:

4-6

INGREDIENTS

8 zucchini, spiralized

4 tbsp butter

2 lbs skinless, boneless chicken

1 tbsp Kosher salt

1 tbsp black pepper

1/2 cup onion, finely chopped

4 garlic cloves, minced

2 cups sliced mushrooms

1 tbsp chopped fresh thyme

1/2 cup chardonnay or white wine vinegar

1/3 cup whipping cream

12 oz bag frozen peas

Chopped parsley for garnish

DIRECTIONS

1. Using a spiralizer or julienne peeler, spiralize zucchini into spaghetti size noodles. Pat dry. Set aside.

2. In a large sauté pan over medium-high heat, melt half the butter. Sprinkle chicken with salt and pepper and cook in until lightly browned. Remove chicken from pan. Cut into 1 inch cubes.

3. To the pan with the drippings, add onions, garlic, mushrooms, thyme, wine, and whipping cream. Simmer for about 5 minutes, or until sauce is thickened.

4. When sauce is at desired thickness, add the frozen peas and take off heat.

5. Gently mix the noodles with the chopped chicken and sauce until well combined. Pour into a casserole dish.

6. Bake at 375 for 25-30 minutes. Cool slightly for ease in cutting.

Apple Chicken Sausages with Rutabagas, Caramelized Red Onions and Radicchio

A hearty European inspired dish bursting with flavor and texture.

PREP TIME:

3 Minutes

COOK TIME:

32 Minutes

TOTAL TIME:

35 Minutes

SERVES:

4

INGREDIENTS

1 tbsp butter

3 tsp olive oil, divided

2 medium red onions, halved and thinly sliced

2 large heads Treviso radicchio, cored and thinly sliced

3 tbsp balsamic vinegar

Pinch salt (optional)

Pinch ground black pepper (optional)

4 cooked chicken-apple sausages (3 oz each)

3 rutabaga, spiralized

DIRECTIONS

1. In a heavy skillet, heat butter with 1 tsp olive oil over medium heat. Add red onions and sauté 15 to 20 minutes, or until soft and golden brown. Add radicchio and sauté 2 minutes, or until wilted. Add balsamic vinegar, increase heat to medium-high and cook 1 to 2 minutes, or until liquid is absorbed. Season with salt and pepper, if using.

2. Meanwhile, using a spiralizer or julienne peeler, spiralize the rutabagas into spaghetti size noodles. Heat remaining 2 tsp olive oil in a large skillet over medium-high heat. On one side of skillet add rutabaga noodles and sauté for 2 to 3 minutes. To the other half of the skillet, add chicken-apple sausages and cook 5 to 7 minutes, or until sausages are well browned and heated through and noodles are tender

3. Serve sausages alongside rutabaga noodles and radicchio mixture.

Chicken Paprikash

This classic dish has rich, full bodied flavor. Often served with the German pasta 'Spaetzel' or with the Hungarian dumpling 'Halousky', this version is served over potato and celeriac noodles.

PREP TIME:

5 Minutes

COOK TIME:

35 Minutes

TOTAL TIME:

40 Minutes

SERVES:

6

INGREDIENTS

5 tablespoons butter, divided

2 tbsp paprika

2 medium onions, sliced

1 whole chicken , quartered

2 cups chicken broth

4 russet potatoes, spiralized

1 celery root, spiralized

1 tbsp vegetable oil

4 tbsp sour cream

3 to 4 tbsp flour (optional)

DIRECTIONS

1. In a Dutch oven, melt 4 tbsp butter over medium-low heat. Stir paprika into butter. Add the onions and sauté the onions 10 to 15 minutes, or until lightly caramelized. Remove onions from pan.

2. Melt the remaining 1 tbsp butter in the Dutch oven. Add chicken. Brown the chicken in the butter, turning often.

3. Add the chicken broth and the sautéed onions to the chicken. Cover and simmer for one hour, or until chicken is fully cooked.

4. Meanwhile, using a spiralizer or julienne peeler, spiralize the potatoes and celeriac into wide (egg noodle size) noodles.

5. In a skillet over medium heat, add vegetable oil. Add the noodles and cook 6 to 8 minutes, or until tender. Add noodles to serving dish.

6. Remove chicken from the Dutch oven and plate with noodles. Stir the sour cream into the gravy in the pan. Add flour to gravy, if using, to thicken to your liking. Pour gravy over chicken and noodles. Serve.

Garlic and Herb Lemon Chicken with Roasted Delicata Squash

For a flavorful, quick and easy week night meal this simple chicken dish is perfect. If you have not tried delicata squash, you will be pleasantly surprised.

PREP TIME:

5 Minutes

COOK TIME:

30 Minutes

TOTAL TIME:

35 Minutes

SERVES:

4

INGREDIENTS

2 medium delicata, spiralized

3 tbsp olive oil, divided

Kosher salt

4 boneless skinless chicken breasts (approximately 1 lb)

1 1/2 tsp parsley flakes

1 tsp seasoned salt

1/2 tsp garlic powder

1/2 tsp ground black pepper

1 tsp dried basil

1 tbsp lemon juice

1 tbsp chopped fresh parsley

DIRECTIONS

1. Heat oven to 400°F.

2. Using a spiralizer or julienne peeler, spiralize the delicata squash into fettuccini size noodles. Place noodles on tinfoil lined baking sheet. Drizzle with 1 1/2 tbsp olive oil, sprinkle with kosher salt.

3. Spray 13x9-inch (3-quart) glass baking dish with cooking spray. Brush both sides of chicken with 1 1/2 tbsp olive oil. Sprinkle both sides with parsley flakes, seasoned salt, garlic pepper and basil. Place in baking dish.

4. Bake chicken uncovered 25 to 35 minutes, or until juice of chicken is no longer pink when centers of thickest pieces are cut.

5. After chicken has been in oven 15 minutes, add baking sheet with delicata squash to the oven. Bake for 10 minutes, turning squash half way through baking time.

6. Place squash onto serving plate. Top with chicken breasts. Drizzle with lemon. Sprinkle with fresh parsley.

COOK'S NOTES:

You do not need to remove the skin from delicata squash, since it is soft and very tasty. Eliminating peeling the delicata makes this recipe so much easier. The added coloring to the delicata noodles makes this dish more festive.

If you want to speed up your meal preparation even more, the roasted chicken can be packaged and refrigerated up to 2 days, or frozen up to 1 month.

You can use butternut squash in place of the delicata, however you will need to increase your baking time 5 to 7 minutes more, or until squash is done to your liking.

Leftover Turkey Tetrazzini

An easy and delicious way to use up your leftover turkey from holiday gatherings.

PREP TIME:

10 Minutes

COOK TIME:

40 Minutes

TOTAL TIME:

50 Minutes

SERVES:

4

INGREDIENTS

1/4 cup butter

1/4 cup all-purpose flour

1/4 tsp salt

1/4 tsp pepper

1 cup chicken broth

1 cup whipping cream

2 cups cubed cooked turkey

1 3 oz can sliced mushrooms, drained

2 tbsp sherry (optional)

4 medium zucchini, spiralized

1/4 cup grated parmesan

DIRECTIONS

1. Preheat oven to 350 degrees.

2. In a large saucepan, melt butter over low heat. Blend in flour and seasonings. Cook over low heat, stirring until mixture is smooth and bubbly. Stir in broth and cream. Heat to boiling, stirring constantly. Boil and stir 1 minute. Remove from heat.

3. Stir in turkey, mushrooms and sherry, if using.

4. Using a spiralizer or julienne peeler, spiralize the zucchini into fettuccine size noodles. Add to sauce mixture.

5. Pour into ungreased 2 quart casserole dish. Sprinkle with parmesan. Bake uncovered 30 minutes or until bubbly. To brown the top, place briefly under broiler, if desired.

Chicken and Tangy Peanut Sauce over Squash and Carrot Noodles

A very colorful combination of vegetables delivers an inviting foundation for the chicken and peanut sauce.

PREP TIME:

10 Minutes

COOK TIME:

5 Minutes

TOTAL TIME:

15 Minutes

SERVES:

3 to 4

INGREDIENTS

1/2 cup peanut butter

1 tbsp soy sauce

3 tbsp rice vinegar

2 tsp sesame oil

1 tsp minced garlic

1/2 tsp granulated sugar

3 medium zucchini, spiralized

3 medium summer squash, spiralized

2 large carrots, spiralized

4 cups diced cooked chicken (approximately 16 oz)

1/4 cup chopped fresh cilantro

2 tbsp sesame seeds

DIRECTIONS

1. In a medium bowl, add the peanut butter, soy sauce, rice vinegar, sesame oil, garlic, and sugar. Mix until well blended. Slowly mix in 1/3 to 1/4 cup of water, or as much as needed to reach your desired consistency. (The spiralized vegetables will also add moisture to your salad.)

2. Using a spiralizer or julienne peeler, spiralize the zucchini, summer squash and carrots into spaghetti size noodles.

3. Blanch the carrots, by adding them to a pot of boiling water for 3 to 5 minutes, drain and immediately plunge into icy cold water to stop the cooking process. Follow the same process for the zucchini and summer squash but boil for 2 to 3 minutes. Once vegetables have cooled, drain thoroughly.

4. In a serving bowl or salad plates, add the vegetable noodles. Top with chicken and drizzle with dressing. Sprinkle cilantro and sesame seeds over top to serve.

Chicken Zucchini Lasagna

Try out this zesty, flavorful lasagna that is gluten free and lighter on the carbohydrates.

PREP TIME:

10 Minutes

COOK TIME:

35 Minutes

TOTAL TIME:

45 Minutes

SERVES:

6

INGREDIENTS

2 1/2 tbsp olive oil, divided

1 small onion, chopped

1/2 tsp red pepper flakes

1 lb ground chicken

1 28 oz can diced tomatoes

3 tbsp chopped fresh oregano

2 tsp salt

2 medium zucchini

1 cup ricotta cheese

DIRECTIONS

1. Preheat the oven to 375°F.

2. In a large skillet heat 2 tbsp of the oil. Add the onion and red pepper flakes and sauté about 6 to 8 minutes, or until onion is soft. Add the chicken and cook 5 to 7 minutes, or until chicken in golden brown and chicken is crumbled. Add the tomatoes and bring the mixture to a boil. Reduce heat to medium and simmer, uncovered, about 20 minutes or until it is spaghetti sauce consistency. Add the oregano and salt and stir. Remove from heat and set aside to cool.

3. Cut off the ends of the zucchini. Using a mandoline, slice the zucchini into thin (1/8 to 1/4 in thick) strips. In the bottom of an 8 in baking dish, layer 5 to 6 zucchini slices. Top with 1 cup of the sauce. Dot with 1/4 cup of the ricotta. Repeat these layers twice. Top with the remaining zucchini and brush the top with the remaining 1/4 teaspoon oil. Dot with the remaining 1/4 cup ricotta. Top with the Parmesan cheese.

4. Bake for 50 to 60 minutes, until the lasagna is bubbling and the top is brown. Let stand for 10 minutes before serving for ease in cutting.

COOK'S NOTE:

This is a wonderful make ahead dish. You can complete all steps through # 4, cover dish tightly with plastic wrap and tinfoil and either refrigerate or freeze. This dish can be frozen for up to 2 months or refrigerated for up to 3 days. The lasagna should be completely thawed before baking. If dish is cold when putting in the oven, you may want to add 10 to 15 minutes to the baking time, or until bubbling around the edge of the dish.

Lemon-Garlic Chicken with Zucchini Noodles

Zucchini noodles get an uplift with delectable lemon and garlic marinated chicken.

PREP TIME:

5 Minutes + 30 minutes marinating time

COOK TIME:

10 Minutes

TOTAL TIME:

15 Minutes

SERVES:

2

INGREDIENTS

1/2 lb chicken breast, cut into strips

1/2 tbsp olive oil

2 garlic cloves, minced

1 1/2 tbsp lemon juice (1/2 lemon)

Zest from 1/2 lemon

1 tbsp minced fresh parsley

1/2 tsp salt

1/4 tsp ground black pepper

2 medium zucchini, spiralized

2 tbsp butter

Pinch sea salt (optional)

Pinch ground black pepper (optional)

Fresh parsley (optional)

DIRECTIONS

1. Mix together olive oil, garlic, lemon juice, zest, parsley, salt and pepper in a small bowl. Add chicken strips. Cover and marinate for 25 to 30 minutes.

2. Using a spiralizer or julienne peeler, spiralize the zucchini into spaghetti size noodles. Set aside.

3. In a medium skillet, heat butter over medium low heat. Remove chicken from marinade and reserve marinade. Add chicken strips and cook for 2 to 4 minutes per side, or until the internal temperature is 165°.

3. Add marinade to skillet. Heat to soft boil. Add zucchini, reduce heat and simmer for 2 to 3 minutes, or until noodles are soft. Sprinkle with salt and pepper, if using. Remove from heat

4. Sprinkle with fresh parsley, if using and serve.

Chicken Tostadas

Great for eating during your favorite football game, these tostadas are festive, packed with flavor and ready in no time.

PREP TIME:

5 Minutes

COOK TIME:

40 Minutes

TOTAL TIME:

45 Minutes

SERVES:

8

INGREDIENTS

8 corn tortillas, 6 inch diameter

2 tbsp vegetable oil

2 cups medium picante sauce

1 rotisserie chicken meat coarsely shredded (approximately 4 cups)

1/2 cup chopped fresh cilantro, divided

3 cups iceberg lettuce, shredded

6 large radishes, spiralized

1 large jicama, spiralized

1/2 medium onion, chopped

1/2 cup chopped fresh cilantro, divided

1 16oz can refried beans

1 avocado halved, pitted, and peeled

1/2 cup sour cream

1/4 cup crumbled queso añjo or Romano cheese

DIRECTIONS

1. Preheat oven to 400°F.

2. Brush the tortillas lightly with the oil. Place in single layer on two cookie sheets. Bake for 5 minutes, turn tortillas and bake for 3 to 6 minutes longer, until the tortillas are crisp and light brown. Transfer to plates.

3. In a large sauce pan, add picante sauce chicken and 1/2 of the cilantro. Heat until warmed through. In a separate pan, heat refried beans.

4. Use a mandoline to shred the lettuce. Using a spiralizer or julienne peeler, spiralize the radishes and jicama into thin curls. Toss together lettuce, radishes, jicama, onions and remaining cilantro.

4. To assemble, spread tortillas thickly with heated refried beans, then top with chicken mixture. Add a dollop of sour cream to each tostada. Mound lettuce mixture on top and sprinkle with queso añjo. Serve.

COOK'S NOTES:

For a festive meal or half time party, serve with Margaritas, chips, salsa and queso.

Chicken, Sweet Potato and Brie Galette

A quick and easy tart filled with chicken and sweet potatoes and then pulled together with creamy, flavorful Brie delivers savory flavors in an elegant package.

PREP TIME:

8 Minutes

COOK TIME:

17 Minutes

TOTAL TIME:

25 Minutes

SERVES:

4

INGREDIENTS

6 oz firm Brie, divided

1 medium sweet potato, spiralized

2 cups shredded rotisserie chicken

1/4 cup chicken broth

1/4 cup walnuts, toasted and chopped

1/4 tsp salt

1/8 tsp ground black pepper

1 9 inch store-bought round pie dough

DIRECTIONS

1. Adjust oven rack to middle position and heat oven to 475 degrees.

2. Cut 4 ounces Brie into 1-inch pieces, including rind. Finely chop remaining 2 ounces Brie.

3. Using a spiralizer or julienne peeler, spiralize the sweet potato into fettuccini size noodles.

4. In a small microwave safe bowl, combine chicken, broth, sweet potato noodles, finely chopped Brie, walnuts, salt and pepper. Cover and microwave 1 to 2 minutes, or until heated through. Remove from microwave and stir.

5. Line a baking sheet with parchment paper. Place pie dough round in center. Spread chicken mixture evenly over dough, leaving 1 1/2 inch edge uncovered. Fold edge of dough over filling, pleating it every 2 to 3 inches. Place 1-inch Brie pieces on top, with rind facing up. Bake tart about 15 minutes, or until crust is golden and cheese is melted. Rotate sheet halfway through baking. Let cool slightly before cutting and serving.

COOK'S NOTES:

Store bought rotisserie chicken makes this dish a snap to prepare. An typical chicken will yield 3 to 4 cups of shredded chicken. You can serve the chicken pieces earlier in the week, reserving 2 cups for this recipe. Alternatively you could refrigerate the remaining shredded chicken for up to 3 days or freeze for up to 3 months.

To toast walnuts, place walnuts on a rimmed baking sheet. Toast in a 350° oven for 5 to 8 minutes, until nuts are brown and fragrant, shaking nuts partway through toasting.

Mediterranean Chicken With Artichoke Hearts and Olives

Artichoke hearts, olives and spices deliver a bounty of Mediterranean tastes to the delicate pairing of chicken and zucchini.

PREP TIME:

5 Minutes

COOK TIME:

12 Minutes

TOTAL TIME:

17 Minutes

SERVES:

4

INGREDIENTS

4 chicken cutlets

1 tablespoon olive oil

3 tablespoons butter

1/2 cup dry white wine

1/2 cup chicken broth

1/3 tsp allspice

3/4 tsp dried basil

1/3 tsp paprika

1 tbsp flour

3 medium zucchini, spiralized

1 cup marinated artichoke hearts, drained

1/3 cup Greek olives, pitted and halved

2 tbsp pine nuts (optional)

DIRECTIONS

1. Heat a large skillet over medium heat. Add olive oil and heat. Add chicken cutlets and cook for about 3 minutes per side, or until chicken is browned and cooked through. Transfer chicken to plate and tent loosely with foil.

2. In pan with drippings, add butter and heat until melted. Add wine and chicken broth. Blend in allspice, basil and paprika. Continue stirring and add in flour.

3. Meanwhile, using a spiralizer or julienne peeler, spiralize the zucchini into fettuccini size noodles. Add to skillet with sauce. Cook 2 to 3 minutes, stirring gently, until sauce begins to thicken and noodles are tender. Remove noodles from sauce and plate.

4. Add artichoke hearts, olives and cooked chicken cutlets. Toss to combine with sauce. Remove from heat and serve mixture over zucchini noodles. Top with pine nuts, if using.

Savory Skillet Turkey Sausage with Potato-Celeriac Noodles

This delectable dish arrives with onions, colorful peppers and garlic to elevate the flavor of sausage and potatoes.

PREP TIME:

8 Minutes

COOK TIME:

24 Minutes

TOTAL TIME:

32 Minutes

SERVES:

3

INGREDIENTS

Cooking spray

14 oz smoked turkey sausage, sliced diagonally

1 tbsp butter

1 tbsp olive oil

1 cup chopped onion

1 cup chopped red bell pepper

1 cup chopped green bell pepper

4 russet potatoes, spiralized

1 small celery root, spiralized

1 garlic clove, minced

1 1/2 cups frozen whole kernel corn, thawed

DIRECTIONS

1. Coat a large skillet or cast iron pan with cooking spray. Heat pan over medium-high heat. Add sausages and sauté for 2 to 3 minutes, or until brown on both sides. Transfer to a plate and tent with foil to keep warm.

2. Add butter and olive oil to skillet. Reduce heat to medium. Add onions and bell peppers and sauté 5 to 7 minutes, or until softened and beginning to brown. Add corn and sausage to mixture and sauté for 4 to 6 minutes more, or until heated through.

3. Meanwhile, using a spiralizer or julienne peeler, spiralize the potatoes and celery root into spaghetti size noodles. Coat a medium skillet with cooking spray and heat over medium heat. Add potato and celery noodles, and garlic to skillet and sauté 6 to 8 minutes, or until they have reached desired tenderness.

4. Plate noodles and serve sausage mixture over the top.

Fish and Seafood Main Dishes

Tuna Noodle Casserole

A traditional comfort food casserole updated with zucchini noodles but with all the great flavor you are accustomed to.

PREP TIME:

20 Minutes

COOK TIME:

45 Minutes

TOTAL TIME:

65 Minutes

SERVES:

8

INGREDIENTS

2 5 oz cans tuna fish

2 medium zucchini, spiralized

1 small onion, chopped

3 garlic cloves, minced

1 celery stalk, chopped

3 tbsp butter, divided

2 tbsp all-purpose flour

1 1/2 cups milk

Salt and Pepper

DIRECTIONS

1. Heat oven to 350 degrees.

2. Using a spiralizer or julienne peeler, spiralize the zucchini into fettuccine size noodles. Put noodles in a medium-size bowl.

3. In a small pan, melt 1 tbsp butter. Add onion, garlic and celery and sauté until onions are golden brown. Add mixture to noodles.

4. In another small pan, melt remaining 2 tbsp butter over low heat. Add flour and whisk until mixture is bubbly. Slowly whisk in milk, stirring continuously, until mixture is thick and bubbly. Remove from heat immediately. Add salt and pepper to taste.

5. Drain tuna and break apart with a fork. Add tuna to zucchini noodles in bowl. Stir to blend.

6. Put tuna mixture into a 9x9 inch casserole dish. Pour the thickened milk and flour sauce over the tuna and noodles. Bake for 45 to 60 min, or until mixture is heated through and bubbly.

Grilled Shrimp with Zucchini Noodles and Lemon Basil Dressing

From the cover, this light and easy main dish can be ready in just minutes.

PREP TIME:

5 Minutes

COOK TIME:

7 Minutes

TOTAL TIME:

12 Minutes

SERVES:

4

INGREDIENTS

Zest from 1 lemon

2 cups fresh basil, chiffonade

1/3 cup toasted sliced almonds, divided

2 garlic cloves, coarsely chopped

1 shallot, coarsely chopped

1/4 tsp red pepper flakes

1/2 cup + 1 tbsp olive oil, divided

1 tbsp red wine vinegar

1 pound shrimp, (26 - 30 count) peeled and de-veined

5 medium-sized zucchini, spiralized

Kosher salt and freshly cracked black pepper

DIRECTIONS

1. In a blender combine lemon zest, basil, 1/4 cup sliced
   almonds, garlic, shallot, red pepper flakes, olive oil and
   red wine vinegar. Blend until smooth. Season with salt
   and pepper, to your liking. set aside.

2. Heat 1 tbsp of olive oil over medium high heat. Add
   shrimp and cook shrimp for 2 to 4 minutes, or until pink
   and fully cooked. Remove from heat. Mix in 2 tbsp of
   the lemon basil dressing.

3. Transfer shrimp, using a slotted spoon, to a serving bowl
   and set aside.

4. Using a spiralizer or julienne peeler, spiralize the
   zucchini into spaghetti size noodles. Add zucchini
   noodles to the same pan used for the shrimp and sauté
   for 1 to 2 minutes over medium heat until just tender.
   Add 2 tbsp of the lemon basil dressing. Toss to coat.
   Remove from heat.

5. Add the shrimp to the top of the zucchini noodles.
   Season with Kosher salt and freshly cracked pepper, if

using. Top with the remaining toasted sliced almonds.
Serve immediately.

COOK'S NOTES:

To chiffonade basil, remove stems and stack 10 or more
leaves together. Roll the leaves lengthwise into a fairly
tight spiral. Cut leaves crosswise into thin strips. Fluff
leaves when done to separate. This method for cutting
basil, is a flavorful and colorful addition to pasta and
salads.

Any remaining Lemon Basil Dressing can be stored in the
refrigerator for up to one week and used in other dishes.

Lemon-Garlic Shrimp with Zucchini Noodles and Spinach

Zucchini noodles offer a lighter pairing with this marinated shrimp than the traditional wheat noodles.

PREP TIME:

25 Minutes

COOK TIME:

5 Minutes

TOTAL TIME:

30 Minutes

SERVES:

2

INGREDIENTS

2 medium zucchini, spiralized

12-15 large shrimp, peeled and deveined

1/2 tbsp olive oil

3 garlic cloves, minced

1 tbsp minced fresh parsley

Zest from 1/2 lemon

Lemon juice from 1/2 lemon

1 tbsp butter or coconut oil

1 1/2-2 cups baby spinach

Kosher salt and fresh ground pepper

DIRECTIONS

1. In a small bowl combine olive oil, garlic, parsley, lemon juice, lemon zest, and salt and pepper. Let sit for about 20 to 30 minutes, or until flavorings meld together.

2. Using a spiralizer or julienne peeler, spiralize the zucchini into spaghetti size noodles. Set aside.

3. Heat butter over medium heat. Add shrimp with marinade and cook for about 30 seconds. Flip the shrimp, cook for another 30 seconds. Remove shrimp from pan with a slotted spoon. Set aside.

4. Add the zucchini noodles to the pan. Add more butter, if needed. Cook for 1 to 2 minutes, or until noodles are very slightly soft.

5. Add spinach and shrimp to the pan with zucchini. Toss in pan about 1 to 2 minutes, or until shrimp is pink and opaque, noodles are soft, and spinach is wilted, Add salt and pepper, if using. Squeeze lemon juice from remaining half of lemon, if desired.

Spicy Shrimp and Parsnip Noodles

A surprising taste pairing of the spicy shrimp seasonings on a bed of sweet parsnips.

PREP TIME:

5 Minutes

COOK TIME:

15 Minutes

TOTAL TIME:

20 Minutes

SERVES:

4

INGREDIENTS

4 large parsnips, spiralized

3 tbsp olive oil, divided

1 cup diced white onion

2 large garlic cloves, minced

1/4 tsp red pepper flakes

1/2 tsp smoked paprika

1/2 tsp chili powder

Kosher salt (optional)

Ground black pepper (optional)

1/2 cup low-sodium chicken broth

1 lb shrimp, (26 – 30 count) cleaned and peeled

2 tbsp freshly chopped parsley (optional)

DIRECTIONS

1. Using a spiralizer or julienne peeler, spiralize the parsnips into wide Tagliatelle-style noodles. Set aside.

2. In a large skillet, heat 2 tbsp olive oil over medium heat. Add the onions and sauté about 3 to 5 minutes, or until onion is translucent. Add the garlic and red pepper flakes and sauté about 2 minutes, or until garlic begins to brown.

3. Add the remaining 1 tbsp olive oil and the parsnip noodles to the skillet. Add the chili powder, smoked paprika, and salt and pepper, if using.

4. Cook for 3 to 4 minutes, until noodles are slightly softened, and then move noodles to the edge of the skillet. Add the chicken broth and shrimp to the middle of the pan. Cook shrimp for 2 minutes; turn shrimp over and cook another 2 minutes, or until shrimp is pink and cooked to desired doneness. Gently toss noodles and shrimp together.

5. Remove from heat and serve immediately. Top with chopped parsley, if using.

Spanish Shrimp and Scallops with Butternut Squash

One of my all-time favorite Spanish dishes is Paella. This dish has all the flavors you would expect in the traditional paella, but is served with butternut squash noodles for a lighter flair.

PREP TIME:

5 Minutes

COOK TIME:

35 Minutes

TOTAL TIME:

40 Minutes

SERVES:

6

INGREDIENTS

2 large butternut squash necks, spiralized

3 tbsp olive oil, divided

3/4 lb jumbo shrimp, peeled and deveined

3/4 lb scallops

1 chorizo sausage, thickly sliced (about 3 oz)

1 medium onion, chopped

2 garlic cloves. minced

1 14.5 oz can diced tomatoes

2 tsp salt

1/4 tsp smoked paprika

1/4 tsp cracked black pepper

Pinch saffron threads (2 to 3 strands)

1 3/4 cups chicken broth

1 cup frozen peas, thawed

4 tbsp fresh parsley (optional)

Lemon wedges for garnish (optional)

DIRECTIONS

1. Using a spiralizer or julienne peeler, spiralize the butternut squash into spaghetti size noodles. Trim to 3 in lengths. Set aside.

2. In a large skillet, heat 2 tbsp olive oil over medium-high heat. Add shrimp to pan and cook for 3 to 5 minutes, turning once, until shrimp is pink on both sides. Transfer shrimp to a plate. Add scallops to skillet and sear for 1 1/2 minutes per side. Transfer scallops to plate with shrimp.

3. Add the chorizo slices to the pan and cook for 2 to 3 minutes, or until sausage begins to brown.

4. Add the remaining 1 tablespoon of oil, onion, garlic, tomatoes, salt, paprika, pepper, and saffron to the sausages in the skillet. Sauté for 5 to 7 minutes, or until the onions are translucent.

5. Add the chicken broth to the skillet, stirring to scrape up the browned bits from the bottom of the skillet. Reduce heat to medium. Stir in the sweet potato noodles and simmer for 7 to 9 minutes, or until squash in just tender and most of the juices have evaporated.

6. Add the shrimp and scallops to the mixture in the skillet. Add peas and cook for 3 to 5 minutes more, until dish is heated through and peas are tender.

7. Sprinkle the parsley over the top, if using. Serve with lemon wedges, if using.

COOK'S NOTES:

For best results, use a Paella pan or a wide shallow pan for cooking and serving.

Traditional paella has a toasted rice bottom called socarrat. This bottom forms with the traditional Arborio rice and with squash noodles. So don't be concerned if your noodles are sticking to the bottom of the pan, as long as they are getting toasted and not burned.

Crab Meat, Asparagus and Kohlrabi

The slightly sweet and buttery taste of kohlrabi combined with succulent crab meat is a feast for your palate.

PREP TIME:

2 Minutes

COOK TIME:

16 Minutes

TOTAL TIME:

18 Minutes

SERVES:

4

INGREDIENTS

4 medium kohlrabi, spiralized

2 tbsp butter

2 tbsp extra-virgin olive oil

4 garlic cloves, minced

1 1/4 cup dry white wine

1 1/2 tbsp lemon juice

3/4 lb asparagus, cut diagonally into 2-in lengths

2 6 oz cans crab meat

1/2 cup chopped fresh Italian parsley

Salt (optional)

Freshly ground black pepper (optional)

Freshly shredded Parmesan cheese (optional)

DIRECTIONS

1. Using a spiralizer or julienne peeler, spiralize the kohlrabi into spaghetti size noodles.

2. In a large skillet, heat the butter and olive oil over medium heat. Add the garlic and sauté until fragrant. Add the wine and lemon juice and simmer for about 10 minutes, or until the liquid is reduced by half.

3. Add the asparagus and kohlrabi to the skillet, cover and steam for 5 to 7 minutes, or until the asparagus is just tender-crisp and the kohlrabi is just soft. Add the crab meat and toss gently until heated through.

4. Add parsley and salt and pepper, using. Toss again. Transfer to a warm serving bowl. Sprinkle with shredded parmesan, if using.

Tilapia and Mustard Cream Sauce over Pasta

Cool lime complements the mustard cream over delicate tilapia and zucchini noodles.

PREP TIME:

10 Minutes

COOK TIME:

12 Minutes

TOTAL TIME:

22 Minutes

SERVES:

2

INGREDIENTS

2 tilapia filets

1 lime, cut in half

Pinch salt

Pinch ground black pepper

3 medium zucchini, spiralized

3/4 cup chicken broth

2 tablespoons Dijon mustard

2 tsp cilantro

1 teaspoon ground cumin

2 tablespoons whipping cream

DIRECTIONS

1. Preheat the oven to 400 degrees.

2. Using a spiralizer or julienne peeler, spiralize the zucchini into wide tagliatelle-size noodles. Set aside on paper towels, if desired.

3. Spray a baking sheet with cooking spray. Place the tilapia filets on a baking sheet. Squeeze each filet lightly with the lime juice. Season with salt and pepper. Bake for 10 to 15 minutes, or until tilapia is opaque and cooked through.

4. While the tilapia is roasting, in a large frying pan add chicken broth, mustard, cilantro and cumin. Whisk ingredients well and bring to a simmer. Add cream and zucchini noodles and simmer for 2 minutes, or until heated through. Remove from heat.

5. Using thongs, transfer zucchini to plates. Top with tilapia. Pour cream sauce over top.

Veggie Tuna Noodle Casserole

A comforting fall dish layered with zucchini noodles and slices for a healthy and hearty meal.

PREP TIME:

30 Minutes

COOK TIME:

35 Minutes

TOTAL TIME:

65 Minutes

SERVES:

6

INGREDIENTS

4 medium zucchini, spiralized

2 medium zucchini, cut into 1/4-inch slices

2 tsp olive oil, divided

1 celery stalk, chopped

1 garlic clove, minced

2 .5oz cans tuna, drained and flaked

1/2 cup sour cream

1/2 cup mayonnaise

4 green onions, thinly sliced

2 tsp Dijon mustard

1/2 tsp dried thyme

1/4 tsp salt

1/4 tsp black pepper

1 cup shredded Monterey Jack cheese

1 medium tomato, chopped (optional)

2 tbsp minced fresh basil (optional)

DIRECTIONS

1. Preheat oven to 375° degrees.

2. Using a spiralizer or julienne peeler, spiralize the zucchini into spaghetti size noodles. Pat dry. Set aside.

3. In a large skillet, sauté zucchini slices in 1 teaspoon oil until crisp-tender. Remove from skillet. Set aside.

4. In the same skillet, sauté celery in remaining oil until crisp-tender. Add garlic, sauté 1 minute, or until garlic is fragrant.

5. In a large bowl, add tuna, sour cream, mayonnaise, green onions, mustard, thyme, salt, pepper and sautéed celery mixture. Mix well. Add in zucchini noodles and toss to combine.

6. In a greased 11 in x 7 in baking dish; add half of the zucchini noodle mixture. Top with half of the sliced zucchini. Repeat layers.

7. Cover and bake at 375° for 30 minutes. Uncover; sprinkle with cheese. Bake 5-10 minutes longer or until cheese is melted. Combine tomato and basil, if using. Sprinkle over top of casserole.

Shrimp with Slow Roasted Tomatoes and Zucchini Linguine

Fresh shrimp and the slightly sweet taste of roasted tomatoes delivers exquisite taste to the zucchini noodles.

PREP TIME:

3 Minute

COOK TIME:

12 Minutes

TOTAL TIME:

15 Minutes

SERVES:

2

INGREDIENTS

2 tbsp olive oil

2 garlic cloves, sliced paper-thin

1 1/2 pounds slow roasted cherry tomatoes

Pinch red pepper flakes

1/2 cup dry white wine

1 lb large shrimp, peeled and deveined

Kosher salt

1 - 1 1/2 cups chicken broth

3 medium zucchini, spiralized

DIRECTIONS

1. Place the olive oil and garlic in a large frying pan over low heat. Cook the garlic slowly for 6 to 8 minutes, or until it is softened, but now browned. Add the tomatoes and red pepper flakes and stir to combine. Cover the pan and let the tomatoes heat slowly for a few minutes.

2. Raise the heat under the frying pan to medium-high. Add the wine just until bubbly and then add the shrimp. Cook for 1 to 3 minutes, or until the shrimp are pink and opaque. With a slotted spoon remove shrimp from pan. Add 1 cup of the chicken broth to the frying pan.

3. Using a spiralizer or julienne peeler, spiralize the zucchini into linguine size noodles. Transfer into the frying pan and gently toss. Cook 2 minutes, or until zucchini noodles are just soft. Add the remaining chicken broth, if necessary to loosen sauce. Add the shrimp back into the pan and toss to mix ingredients and rewarm shrimp, if necessary.

4. Transfer the dressed pasta to warmed shallow individual bowls and serve immediately.

COOK'S NOTE:

Be very careful not to overcook the shrimp. They will become rubbery and lose their delicate flavor.

Delicata Squash Spirals with Tuna, Olives, and Capers

The only thing you will love more than eating delicata squash is preparing it – super easy to work with and a beautiful presentation too.

PREP TIME:

5 Minutes

COOK TIME:

6 Minutes

TOTAL TIME:

11 Minutes

SERVES:

3

INGREDIENTS

1/4 cup olive oil

1/2 cup chopped parsley

2 garlic cloves, minced

1/4 tsp salt

1/4 tsp fresh grated pepper

4 tbsp lemon juice

1 tbsp fresh basil chopped

5 tbsp chopped kalamata olives

2 tbsp capers drained

2/3 cup grated parmesan cheese, divided

1 lemon grated zest (optional)

1 1/2 tbsp olive oil

3 delicata squash, spiralized

1 - 14 oz can tuna in olive oil, drained

DIRECTIONS

1. Combine olive oil, parsley, garlic, salt, pepper, lemon juice, basil, olives, capers, 1/2 cup parmesan, and lemon zest, if using. Break the tuna into large chunks and mix in with other ingredients. Toss carefully Set aside.

2. Using a spiralizer or julienne peeler, spiralize the unpeeled delicata squash into wide (tagliatelle size) noodles.

3. In a large skillet, heat olive oil over medium heat. Add squash and sauté 4 to 6 minutes, or until softened.

4. Add delicata noodles to tuna mixture and toss gently.

5. Sprinkle with remaining parmesan cheese. Serve at room temperature.

Salmon with Creamy Dill Sauce and Celery Root Noodles

Celery root noodles adds a new dimension to salmon paired with a refreshing dill sauce.

PREP TIME:

5 Minutes

COOK TIME:

32 Minutes

TOTAL TIME:

37 Minutes

SERVES:

4

INGREDIENTS

3 celery root bulbs, peeled and spiralized

1 lb fresh salmon, cut into 4 evenly sized pieces

2 tbsp olive oil

Pinch sea salt

Pinch freshly ground black pepper

6 oz Greek plain yogurt

1 tbsp chopped fresh dill weed

1/2 teaspoon grated lemon peel

1 tablespoon lemon juice

1/8 teaspoon pepper

DIRECTIONS

1. Preheat oven to 375 degrees. Bring a large pot of water to a boil.

2. Place salmon in a glass baking dish skin side down. Brush olive oil over salmon. Season with salt and pepper. Bake for 20 to 25 minutes, or until salmon flakes easily with a fork.

3. Using a spiralizer or julienne peeler, spiralize the celery root into spaghetti size noodles. When salmon is almost done, place the celery root noodles into the boiling water and cook for 6 to 7 minutes, or until noodles are tender. Drain.

4. Meanwhile, in a small bowl, mix yogurt, dill weed, lemon peel, lemon juice and pepper. Mix well.

5. Plate cooked celery root and drizzle with 1/2 of dill sauce. Place salmon on noodles. Serve immediately with remaining dill sauce for top of salmon.

Creamy Tuna Noodle Cazuela

The rich and spicy-sweet flavor of piquillo peppers adds just the right amount of Spanish influence to this quick and easy classic tuna noodle dish.

PREP TIME:

4 Minutes

COOK TIME:

21 Minutes

TOTAL TIME:

25 Minutes

SERVES:

4

INGREDIENTS

3 medium yellow squash, spiralized

4 tbsp butter, divided

1 medium onion, finely chopped

2 tbsp flour

3 cups half-and-half

1 1/2 cups frozen baby peas

3/4 cup roasted piquillo peppers, sliced (about 6 oz)

1/2 cup grated Parmigiano-Reggiano cheese

1 6 oz can tuna in oil, drained and flaked

Pinch salt

Pinch ground black pepper

1/2 cup panko

DIRECTIONS

1. Preheat oven to 450°.

2. Using a spiralizer or julienne peeler, spiralize the squash into fettuccine size noodles.

3. In a large saucepan, melt 3 tbsp of the butter. Add the onion and cook over medium-high heat 3 to 4 minutes, or until onions are softened. Add the flour and cook, stirring, for 1 minute. Add the half and half and bring to a boil. Add the squash noodles. Reduce heat and simmer, stirring occasionally, 4 to 6 minutes, or sauce is thickened and noodles are tender. Remove from heat.

4. Add the frozen baby peas, sliced piquillo peppers, Parmigiano-Reggiano cheese, tuna, salt and pepper. Mix gently. Transfer the mixture to a 9-in square glass or ceramic baking dish.

5. In a small skillet, melt the remaining 1 tbsp of butter. Add the panko and toss to combine. Sprinkle the panko over the casserole. Bake for 10 minutes, or until bubbling and golden brown. Serve.

Vegetarian Main Dishes

Zucchini Noodles with Tomato and Pesto

Blended basil, garlic and parmesan pesto adds robust flavor to this light-on-calories pasta dish.

PREP TIME:

10 Minutes

TOTAL TIME:

10 Minutes

SERVES:

4

INGREDIENTS

1 cup packed fresh basil

1 clove garlic

1/4 cup fresh grated parmesan cheese

Kosher salt

Cracked fresh pepper

3 tbsp extra virgin olive oil

3 medium zucchini, spiralized

1 cup cherry tomatoes, halved

Kosher salt, optional

Cracked fresh pepper, optional

DIRECTIONS

1. In a food processor, blend basil, garlic, parmesan cheese, salt and pepper until smooth. Slowly add the olive oil while pulsing. Set aside.

2. Using a spiralizer or julienne peeler, spiralize the zucchini into spaghetti size noodles. Add to salad bowl.

3. Add the pesto and tomatoes to the zucchini and toss until coated. Season with salt and pepper, if using.

Spaghetti alla Carbonara

This classic dish is always a favorite. Making it with the zucchini noodles, you eliminate the wheat pasta but don't sacrifice the taste.

PREP TIME:

5 Minutes

COOK TIME:

15 Minutes

TOTAL TIME:

20 Minutes

SERVES:

2

INGREDIENTS

2 medium zucchini, spiralized

4 eggs, room temperature

1/4 cup milk

1 tbsp olive oil or coconut oil

3 cloves garlic, minced

Freshly ground black pepper (optional)

Grated parmesan cheese (optional)

Fresh parsley (optional)

DIRECTIONS

1. Using a spiralizer or julienne peeler, spiralize the zucchini into spaghetti size noodles.

2. In a bowl, whisk together your eggs, milk and a pinch of black pepper if using.

3. Add the olive oil to a medium sized frying pan and heat to medium. Add the minced garlic sauté for 1 to 2 minutes.

4. Add your zucchini noodles to the pan and cook 3 to 5 minutes, or until noodles are cooked but not too soft.

5. Remove the pan from the heat. Add the egg and milk mixture and stir quickly to coat the noodles. Stir in pan until eggs are cooked.

6. Garnish with grated parmesan cheese and parsley, if using.

Squash Noodles with Sautéed Spinach and Mushrooms

The creamy soft goodness of a delicate fall squash is topped with a light sauce of spinach, mushrooms and garlic.

PREP TIME:

10 Minutes

COOK TIME:

10 Minutes

TOTAL TIME:

20 Minutes

SERVES:

3

INGREDIENTS

2 medium delicata squash (sweet potato squash)

Olive oil

1 large leek, thinly sliced

3 garlic cloves, minced

6 oz fresh mushrooms, sliced

12 oz baby spinach

1/2 cup chicken stock

1/8 cup dry white wine (optional)

Salt and pepper (optional)

DIRECTIONS

1. Using a spiralizer or julienne peeler, spiralize the delicata squash into spaghetti size noodles. Set aside.

2. In a large frying pan, sauté the garlic and leek in olive oil for 2 minutes. Add mushrooms and continue to sauté until mushrooms are softened and lightly browned.

4. Add spinach to pan and pour in chicken stock. Stir the spinach until wilted. Add white wine, if using. Season with salt and pepper, if using.

5. Add delicata squash and stir to combine. Sauté for a few minutes, or until desired doneness.

6. Remove from heat and serve immediately.

Zucchini and Carrot Wrap with Feta and Avocado

Creamy goodness paired with crunchy vegetables yields a wrap that is delicious and satisfying.

PREP TIME:

10 Minutes

COOK TIME:

0 Minutes

TOTAL TIME:

10 Minutes

SERVES:

1

INGREDIENTS

1 medium tortilla wrap (6 to 8 in)

2 tbsp hummus

1/4 avocado, sliced

Salt (optional)

Black pepper (optional)

1 small carrot, spiralized

1/4 cup black beans, drained and rinsed

1/2 small zucchini, spiralized

3 tbsp crumbled feta cheese

DIRECTIONS

1. Spread hummus evenly on tortilla to within 3/4 inch of the edge. Add avocado. Season with salt and pepper, if using.

2. Using a spiralizer or julienne peeler, spiralize the carrots into spaghetti size noodles. Place carrots on top of hummus. Top with black beans.

3. Using a spiralizer or julienne peeler, spiralize the zucchini into spaghetti size noodles. Place on top of black beans. Sprinkle feta on top of zucchini.

4. Roll the wrap up. Secure with toothpicks. Cut in half at an angle to make 2 wraps.

COOK'S NOTE:

To make your tortilla easier to eat, especially if you are on the go, lay a piece of parchment or wax paper under the tortilla. After filling and rolling the tortilla, wrap paper around rolled tortilla. Cut in half (through the paper). Peel back the paper as you eat.

Sweet Potato Noodle Bolognese

A richly flavored Bolognese highlights the sweet toasted flavors of the sweet potato noodles. A special technique to sauté mushrooms adds meaty texture and rich flavor.

PREP TIME:

10 Minutes

COOK TIME:

25 Minutes

TOTAL TIME:

35 Minutes

SERVES:

4 - 6

INGREDIENTS

1/3 cup olive oil, divided

1 medium onion, coarsely chopped

2 garlic cloves, minced

1 celery stalk, chopped

1 carrot, chopped

1 lb button mushrooms, finely chopped

12 oz shiitake mushrooms, stems discarded, caps finely chopped

1/4 cup tomato paste

1 28-ounce can crushed tomatoes

1/4 cup fresh parsley, chopped

8 fresh basil leaves, chopped

1 tbsp oregano flakes

4 medium sweet potatoes, spiralized

Olive oil cooking spray

2 tsp garlic powder

Salt

Freshly ground black pepper

1/4 cup freshly grated Pecorino Romano

DIRECTIONS

1. In a large skillet, heat 2 tbsp of the olive oil. Add the onion and garlic and sauté over medium heat 6 to 8 minutes, or until the onions become very soft. Add the celery and carrot and sauté for 5 minutes more. Transfer mixture to a large saucepan and wipe out skillet.

2. Increase heat to medium- high and add remaining olive oil. When oil starts to shimmer, add button and shiitake mushrooms and cook, stirring occasionally, until mushroom liquid completely evaporates and mushrooms are well-browned all over, about 20 minutes. Add tomato paste and stir to combine. Add canned tomatoes

and cook, scraping up the browned bits on the bottom of the pan. Add mixture to saucepan with the vegetables. Add parsley and basil and cook over medium low heat approximately 30 minutes, or until the sauce thickens.

3. While the sauce is cooking, spiralize the sweet potatoes into spaghetti size noodles using a spiralizer or julienne peeler,. Add the sweet potato noodles to a large skillet over medium heat. Lightly spray the noodles with cooking spray and season with salt, pepper and garlic powder. Toss frequently for 6 to 8 minutes, or until noodles have softened. Remove from heat.

4. When the sauce is done, add the cooked sweet potato noodles to the sauce and toss to combine.

5. Plate the noodles into bowls and top with the Pecorino-Romano.

Zucchini Fettuccine with Butternut Rosemary Sauce

The creamy goodness of butternut squash with onions, garlic and rosemary richly marry with mushrooms and zucchini.

PREP TIME:

5 Minutes

COOK TIME:

55 Minutes

TOTAL TIME:

60 Minutes

SERVES:

4

INGREDIENTS

1 medium butternut squash

3 tbsp olive oil, divided

1 medium onion, chopped

2 garlic cloves, minced

Pinch of fresh rosemary

1 cup whipping cream or half and half

1/2 cup chicken broth

1/2 tsp salt

16 oz portabella mushrooms, sliced

5 medium zucchini, spiralized

Fresh ground black pepper (optional)

DIRECTIONS

1. Preheat oven to 375 degrees.

2. Slice butternut squash in half lengthwise. Remove seeds. Place butternut squash (cut side down) on baking sheet covered with tinfoil.

3. Roast for 45 to 55 minutes, until squash is tender when squeezed and juices are beginning to run on baking sheet. Cool squash. When cool, scoop out squash and add to blender.

4. In a small pan, heat 1 tbsp of olive oil over medium heat. Add onions and garlic and sauté for 3 to 5 minutes, until onion is translucent.

5. Add the onions, garlic rosemary, whipping cream and chicken broth to the squash. Blend until smooth.

6. Add the remaining tablespoon of olive oil to a large pan. Add the mushrooms and sauté for about 3 to 5 minutes, or until softened.

7. Using a spiralizer or julienne peeler, spiralize the zucchini into fettuccini size noodles. Add the zucchini

fettuccine to the mushrooms and sauté 3 minutes. Add the sauce to the pan and continue to cook for 3 to 5 minutes, or until sauce is hot and zucchini is tender.

8. Garnish with freshly-ground black pepper, if using.

Lentil Marinara with Zucchini Spaghetti

A vegetarian version of a traditional spaghetti and meat sauce.

PREP TIME:

10 Minutes

COOK TIME:

45 Minutes

TOTAL TIME:

50 Minutes

SERVES:

4

INGREDIENTS

1 cup dried French lentils, washed and drained

3 cups water

2 tbsp olive oil, divided

1 medium onion, diced

2 garlic cloves, minced

2-15 oz cans, tomato sauce

1 tsp dried basil

1 tsp dried oregano

1/2 tsp dried thyme

Salt (optional)

Ground black pepper (optional)

6 medium zucchini, spiralized

Fresh grated parmesan cheese (optional)

DIRECTIONS

1. Add lentils and 3 cups of water to a medium pot. Bring to a boil and then reduce to simmer. Cover and simmer 45 to 60 minutes, or until lentils are tender. Drain excess liquid.

2. Add 1 tablespoon olive oil to a pan over medium heat. Add the onion and sauté for 5 minutes, or until translucent. Add the garlic and sauté for 1 minute more.

3. Add the tomato sauce, basil, oregano and thyme. Add salt and pepper, if using. Simmer on low for 20 minutes.

4. Add cooked lentils to the tomato sauce and simmer for 5 to 10 minutes, or until smooth.

5. Using a spiralizer or julienne peeler, spiralize the zucchini into spaghetti size noodles.

6. Add 1 tbsp olive oil to a frying pan. Over medium heat, add the zucchini to the oil and sauté for 3 to 5, or until done to your liking.

7. Plate the zucchini. Serve with lentil marinara sauce. Top with parmesan, if using.

Cook's Notes:

For best results, use green lentils (French lentils) because the will stay firmer when cooked and have a nuttier flavor.

Spaghetti with Butter-Roasted Tomato Sauce

You may never eat another sauce after trying this simple, deeply flavored roasted tomato sauce with added character from a surprise ingredient.

PREP TIME:

5 Minutes

COOK TIME:

45 Minutes

TOTAL TIME:

50 Minutes

SERVES:

4

INGREDIENTS

1 28-ounce can crushed tomatoes

8 garlic cloves, crushed

2 anchovy fillets packed in oil

1/4 cup (1/2 stick) unsalted butter, cut into small pieces

1/2 tsp crushed red pepper flakes (optional more for serving)

Kosher salt

Freshly ground black pepper

1/2 cup vegetable broth

1 butternut squash, spiralized

Finely grated Parmesan

DIRECTIONS

1. Preheat oven to 425degrees.

2. Combine in a 13x9 inch baking dish tomatoes, garlic, anchovies, butter, and 1/2 teaspoon red pepper flakes. Season with salt and black pepper.

3. Roast the mixture for 35 to 40 minutes, until the garlic is very soft and the mixture is thick and viscous. Gently toss the mixture halfway through roasting. Add mixture and vegetable broth to large sauce pan.

4. Using a spiralizer or julienne peeler, spiralize the potatoes into fettuccine size noodles. Add to tomato sauce mixture in pan.

5.Cook over medium heat 5 to 7 minutes, until noodles are al dente and sauce coats pasta. Serve. Top with Parmesan cheese and red pepper flakes, if using.

COOK'S NOTES:

The tomato sauce can be made ahead of time. Let cool, cover and refrigerate up to 4 days. Do not make squash noodles ahead of time. Reheat sauce before mixing with pasta.

Zucchini Fettuccine with Peas and Sage Sauce

A savory blend of sage, peas add a delectable flavor to this warm buttery dish.

PREP TIME:

2 Minutes

COOK TIME:

10 Minutes

TOTAL TIME:

12Minutes

SERVES:

4

INGREDIENTS

1/2 cup butter

12 fresh sage leaves

1 cup frozen petite peas

Pinch salt

Pinch freshly ground black pepper

5 zucchini, spiralized

1 1/2 cups grated Parmesan cheese

DIRECTIONS

1. Preheat the oven to 325 degrees.

2. In a small saucepan over medium heat melt 1/4 cup of the butter. Add the sage leaves and cook until they are crisp. When the butter begins to brown, add the peas and cook for 1 minute. Add 1/4 cup water, cover the saucepan and reduce the heat to low. Cook for 7 minutes. Season with salt and pepper.

3. Using a spiralizer or julienne peeler, spiralize the zucchini into fettuccine size noodles. Pat dry with a paper towel. In Melt remaining 1/4 cup butter in a sauté pan Add the zucchini and cook 1 to 2 minutes, or until zucchini is just softened. Add 3/4 cup of the grated Parmesan and the pea-and-sage mixture and toss to coat.

4. Transfer to an ovenproof dish and place in the oven for 5 minutes. Sprinkle with the remaining Parmesan.

Zucchini Fettuccine with Rosemary Butternut Cream Sauce

A satisfying creamy fall dish that is bursting with vegetables and the distinctive taste of rosemary.

PREP TIME:

10 Minutes

COOK TIME:

60 Minutes

TOTAL TIME:

70 Minutes

SERVES:

6

INGREDIENTS

1 butternut squash, medium

2 tbsp olive oil

1 medium onion, chopped

2 garlic cloves, minced

2 tbsp dried rosemary

1 cup whipping cream

1/2 cup chicken broth

1/4 tsp salt

1 lb cremini mushrooms, sliced

7 medium zucchini, spiralized

Pinch freshly ground black pepper (optional)

DIRECTIONS

1. Preheat oven to 375 degrees.

2. Slice butternut squash in half lengthwise. Place butternut squash, cut side down, on baking sheet. Bake for 40 to 50 minutes, until squash is tender and caramelized juices begin to appear on baking sheet. When squash is slightly cooled, scoop out inner meat and add to a blender.

3. In a skillet over medium heat, add 1 tbsp olive oil and the onions. Sauté for 3 to 4 minutes, or until onion is translucent. Add garlic and sauté for 1 to 2 minutes more, or until garlic is just golden.

4. Add the onions, garlic, rosemary, whipping cream, broth and salt to the blender with the squash. Blend until smooth. Set aside.

5. Add the remaining tablespoon of olive oil and the mushrooms to a skillet and sauté for 2 to 4 minutes, or until slightly browned.

6. While mushrooms are cooking, use a spiralizer or julienne peeler to cut the zucchini into fettuccine size noodles. Add noodles to the mushrooms and cook for 2

minutes. Add the butternut squash sauce and cook 2 to 4 minutes, or until zucchini is tender and sauce is hot.

7. Garnish with freshly-ground black pepper, if using. Serve immediately.

Roasted Sweet Potato, Butternut Squash and Asparagus Pasta

Roasting highlights the sweetness and texture of the sweet potato and squash and creates a colorful, delectable dish.

PREP TIME:

10 Minutes

COOK TIME:

30 Minutes

TOTAL TIME:

40 Minutes

SERVES:

4

INGREDIENTS

2 small zucchinis, spiralized

2 sweet potatoes, spiralized

1 large butternut squash, peeled

1 bunch asparagus, cut into 2 in lengths

4 tbsp olive oil, divided

Kosher salt

1/2 cup shredded Monterey Jack

1/3 cup white wine

DIRECTIONS

1. Preheat oven to 400 degrees.

2. Using a spiralizer or julienne peeler, spiralize the zucchini into spaghetti size noodles. Set aside.

3. Spiralize the sweet potato and the neck of the butternut squash into spaghetti size noodles. Remove the seeds from the bulb end of the squash and chop into 1 inch cubes.

4. Place asparagus and butternut squash cubes on baking sheet. Drizzle with 2 tbsp olive oil and toss to coat. Sprinkle generously with salt and roast for 25 minutes, or until tender but crisp.

5. In a skillet over medium heat, add 2 tbsp olive oil and sweet potato and squash noodles. Sauté 4 to 6 minutes, or until noodles are just softening. Add wine, cheese and zucchini noodles. Toss to coat. Cook 2 minutes more until cheese is melted and all noodles are desired consistency. Remove from heat.

6. Add roasted asparagus and butternut squash cubes to top of noodles. Serve immediately.

Spring Ramp Carbonara

Delicate, garlicky and pungent ramps and loads of pancetta adorn zucchini pasta which is crowned by sweet, buttery and nutty grated cheese varieties.

PREP TIME:

5 Minutes

COOK TIME:

16 Minutes

TOTAL TIME:

21 Minutes

SERVES:

4

INGREDIENTS

6 medium yellow squash, spiralized

2 tbsp olive oil

1 cup chopped pancetta

1/3 cup white wine

1/4 cup chicken broth

1 lb ramps

5 eggs

1/2 cup grated Parmesan

1/4 cup grated Pecorino Romano

Pinch freshly ground black pepper (optional)

DIRECTIONS

1. Using a spiralizer or julienne peeler, spiralize the squash into spaghetti size noodles. Set aside.

2. In a large skillet over medium heat add. the olive oil and heat. Add the pancetta and cook 3 to 5 minutes, or until crisp. Add the white wine and cook until reduced by half. Using a slotted spoon, remove the pancetta and set aside. Add chicken broth to the skillet.

3. Separate the ramp bulbs from the leaves. Coarsely chop the bulbs. Add the ramp bulbs to the same skillet and sauté for 4 to 6 minutes, or until soft. Slice the ramp leaves lengthwise into thin ribbons. Add the ramp leaves and sauté for 2 to 4 minutes, or until softly wilted. Add the squash to the skillet, toss to coat and cook 3 to 5 minutes, or until squash noodles are beginning to soften.

4. Meanwhile, in a medium mixing bowl whisk together the eggs, Parmesan and Pecorino Romano cheese.

5. Pour the egg and cheese mixture into the skillet. Quickly and gently toss ingredients together. Remove from heat and stir 1 to 2 minutes, or until the sauce has thickened and the eggs are cooked to your liking. Season with pepper, if using. Serve immediately.

COOK'S NOTE:

Look for ramps in late spring at your farmer's market or local grocery. They are available for a very short time frame, so you should plan ahead and keep your eye out for them.

Spinach and Eggplant Zucchini Lasagna

Great as a make ahead dish, this heavenly lasagna will is loaded with fresh vegetables, zesty seasonings and cheese.

PREP TIME:

15 Minutes

COOK TIME:

70 Minutes

TOTAL TIME:

85 Minutes

SERVES:

8 - 10

INGREDIENTS

Cooking spray

2 medium zucchini, cut lengthwise into 6 slices

2 medium eggplant, peeled and cut lengthwise into 8 slices

1/4 cup + 4 tbsp olive oil, divided

Salt

Ground black pepper

1 medium onion, chopped

2 cloves garlic, minced

1 26 oz. jar chunky pasta sauce

1 teaspoon dried Italian seasoning

1/4 cup chopped fresh basil leaves, divided

1 15 oz. container ricotta cheese

1/2 cup grated Parmesan cheese

1 large egg, lightly beaten

2 cups shredded mozzarella cheese

1 5 oz. package cheese and garlic croutons, crushed

DIRECTIONS

1. Heat oven to 425°F. Coat two 15 x 10 x 1-inch baking pans with cooking spray. Cut the zucchini an eggplant using a mandoline for even slices. Arrange the zucchini and eggplant on baking sheets. Brush tops with 1/4 cup olive oil. Season with salt and pepper. Bake 12 to 15 minutes or until fork tender. Remove from oven. Reduce oven temperature to 375°F.

2. In a large skillet heat 1 tbsp olive oil over medium heat, add onion and garlic and cook 3 to 5 minutes, or until onion is tender. Stir in pasta sauce, Italian seasoning and 3 tablespoons basil. Remove from heat.

3. In a medium bowl, mix ricotta cheese, parmesan cheese and egg until blended.

4. Coat a 13 x 9 inch baking dish with cooking spray. Layer half of eggplant in baking dish. Top with half of ricotta cheese mixture, half of zucchini, 1 1/2 cups pasta sauce mixture and 1 cup mozzarella cheese. Top with remaining eggplant, ricotta mixture, zucchini and pasta sauce mixture.

5.Bake for 30 to 35 minutes or until hot and bubbly. Remove from oven.

6. In a small bowl, Combine crushed croutons and remaining 2 tablespoons olive oil. Toss to coat. Stir in remaining 1 cup mozzarella cheese. Sprinkle evenly over top. Bake an additional 5 to 10 minutes, until cheese is melted and croutons are lightly toasted. Remove from oven; let stand 10 minutes before cutting and serving. Sprinkle with remaining 1 tablespoon basil and serve.

COOK'S NOTES:

Use a mandoline to cut the eggplant and zucchini into even strips. Your task will be easier and the slices will cook evenly.

This is a wonderful make ahead dish. The lasagna can be cut into individual servings and refrigerated for up to 5 days or frozen up to 2 months.

CHAPTER 3
Side Dishes

Spicy Shoe String Jicama Fries

Butternut Squash Noodles with Sun Dried Tomatoes

Caprese Beet Noodle Pasta

Crispy Baked Shoestring Sweet Potato Fries

Zucchini Pasta with Pine Nuts and Cranberries

Potato Noodles Au Gratin

Summer Squash Galette

Sweet and Savory Vegetarian and Gluten-free Kugel

Sweet Potato Pizza Pie

Delicata Squash with Rosemary, Sage and Apple Cider Glaze

Roasted Squash Focaccia

Spicy Shoe String Jicama Fries

Jicama makes a unique, sweet and crispy shoe string fry that is a wonderful alternative to potatoes.

PREP TIME:

10 Minutes

COOK TIME:

35 Minutes

TOTAL TIME:

45 Minutes

SERVES:

5

INGREDIENTS

1 large jicama, peeled and spiralized

2 tbsp olive oil

Salt, to taste

1 tbsp onion powder

2 tsp Hungarian paprika

1 tsp cumin

DIRECTIONS

1. Preheat oven to 400 degrees.

2. Using a spiralizer or julienne peeler, spiralize jicama into fettuccine size noodles and cut into 6 inch (approximately) lengths.

3. Cover 2 large baking pans with tinfoil (optional). Place jicama onto baking pans. Drizzle with olive oil. Toss to evenly coat noodles with oil.

4. Season with salt, onion powder, paprika and cumin. Toss to coat evenly with seasoning. Spread out jicama strings to avoid crowding.

5. Bake for 15 minutes, open oven and turn jicama over and bake for 10-15 minutes more, or until they are cooked to your liking. Remove from oven and serve immediately.

COOK'S NOTE: Covering your baking pans with tinfoil will make cleaning of your pans much easier. You could also use just one baking pan and repeat steps 3 to 5 and replace the tinfoil before making your second batch.

Butternut Squash Noodles with Sun Dried Tomatoes

Sun dried tomatoes and Herbs de Provence add an extra touch to this fall favorite squash.

PREP TIME:

10 Minutes

COOK TIME:

0 Minutes

TOTAL TIME:

10 Minutes

SERVES:

4

INGREDIENTS

4 medium tomatoes

1/2 cup sun dried tomatoes, in oil

2 garlic cloves

1 lemon juice

1 tsp Herbs de Provence

1/2 tsp sea salt

1/4 tsp ground black pepper

1/2 cup avocado oil

2 butternut squash, peeled and spiralized

DIRECTIONS

1. Add fresh tomatoes, sun dried tomatoes, garlic, lemon juice, dried herbs, salt, and pepper into a food processor.

2. Process on high for 30 seconds, scraping sides down as necessary.

3. Drizzle avocado oil on top of mixture and process 60 seconds or until smooth and creamy.

4. Using a spiralizer or julienne peeler, spiralize the butternut squash into spaghetti size noodles.

5. Add to dressing to butternut squash and toss gently. Serve immediately.

Caprese Beet Noodle Pasta

Roasted beets and tomatoes combine with mozzarella in a warm and inviting dish that makes a great side dish or light lunch.

PREP TIME:

10 Minutes

COOK TIME:

20 Minutes

TOTAL TIME:

30 Minutes

SERVES:

1

INGREDIENTS

2 medium beets, spiralized

Olive oil

Salt and pepper (optional)

5 cherry tomatoes, halved

1 garlic clove, thinly sliced

3-4 mini balls of mozzarella cheese

1 tbsp fresh chopped parsley (optional)

DIRECTIONS

1. Preheat oven to 400 degrees.

2. Using a spiralizer or julienne peeler, spiralize the beets into spaghetti size noodles. Set aside.

3. Cover baking sheet with tin foil. Place the tomatoes, seed side up at one end of the baking sheet. Drizzle with olive oil. Sprinkle with salt and pepper, if using. Bake for 5 minutes.

3. Add beets to the other end of the baking sheet with the tomatoes. Spread out loosely. Drizzle with olive oil. Sprinkle with salt and pepper, if using. Return to oven and bake for 5 - 7 minutes more, until beets have softened and darkened slightly.

4. On baking sheet, drop mozzarella balls on top of beets. Return to oven for 2 more minutes.

5. Remove vegetables from oven. Place noodles and mozzarella into a bowl and top with the roasted tomatoes. Garnish with chopped parsley, if using.

Crispy Baked Shoestring Sweet Potato Fries

PREP TIME:

5 Minutes

COOK TIME:

15 Minutes

TOTAL TIME:

20 Minutes

SERVES:

2

INGREDIENTS

1 large sweet potato

2 tbsp olive oil

PINCH SEA SALT

DIRECTIONS

1. Preheat oven to 400 degrees

2. Using a spiralizer or julienne peeler, spiralize the sweet potatoes into spaghetti size noodles.

3. Place noodles on a baking sheet covered with parchment paper. Drizzle olive oil over top and toss so noodles are coated. Sprinkle with sea salt.

4. Bake for 15 to 20 minutes, or until crispy, turning once halfway through baking.

Zucchini Pasta with Pine Nuts and Cranberries

This quick and easy dish is great as a light meal or as a side dish that goes well with just about anything.

PREP TIME:

5 Minutes

COOK TIME:

10 Minutes

TOTAL TIME:

15 Minutes

SERVES:

2

INGREDIENTS

4 zucchini, spiralized

1/2 cup pine nuts, toasted

2 tbsp olive oil

1/4 cup fresh cranberries

Pinch sea salt

DIRECTIONS

1. Using a spiralizer or julienne peeler, spiralize the zucchini into spaghetti size noodles.

2. Put the nuts in a dry skillet and cook over medium-low heat, stirring frequently, approximately 3 minutes, or until golden. Remove nuts from pan and set aside.

3. Add olive oil to skillet. Sauté zucchini for 1 to 2 minutes on medium heat, or until zucchini is lightly cooked.

4. Increase heat to medium high. Add in the pine nuts and cranberries. Sauté for 2 to 3 minutes, until cranberries are slightly popping open and zucchini is soft and golden brown. Add sea salt, if using.

Potato Noodles Au Gratin

A quick and easy recipe that makes an excellent accompaniment to beef, pork and chicken.

PREP TIME:

5 Minutes

COOK TIME:

60 Minutes

TOTAL TIME:

65 Minutes

SERVES:

4

INGREDIENTS

4 large russct potatoes, spiralized

Salt

Ground Pepper

8 tbsp cream cheese

4 tbsp butter

2 cups grated sharp cheddar cheese, divided

1/2 cup half and half

1 1/2 tbsp garlic powder

2 tsp onion powder

1/2 cup grated parmesan (optional)

2 green onions, white and light green parts sliced

DIRECTIONS

1. Preheat oven to 425 degrees.

2. Using a spiralizer or julienne peeler, spiralize the potatoes into spaghetti size noodles.

2. Grease a 2 1/2 to 3 quart casserole dish. Add noodles and season with salt and pepper.

3. In a large pan, melt cream cheese and butter on medium heat.

4. Slowly add milk, stirring continuously.

5. Add half of the grated cheddar cheese, and all of the garlic powder and onion powder to the pan. Stir until melted and well blended. Remove from heat.

6. Spoon cream sauce over potatoes. Cover with tinfoil.

7. Bake for 35 minutes.

8. Remove foil and add remaining cheddar cheese to the top of the potatoes. Sprinkle with parmesan, if using. Bake an additional 20 to 25 minutes, until potatoes are soft and cheese is bubbly. Sprinkle green onions over the top and serve.

COOK'S NOTE:

This recipe can be prepared and baked ahead of time. Cool to room temperature, cover with plastic wrap or aluminum foil and refrigerate for up to 2 days. Rewarm uncovered in a 350°F oven for about 30 to 40 minutes.

If you want to lighten the amount of cheese in this recipe, substitute nutritional yeast for the parmesan.

Summer Squash Galette

Colorful zucchini and yellow squash imparts this rustic free form tart with flavor and beautiful presentation your guest will love.

PREP TIME:

Active: 5 Marinating: 30 Minutes

COOK TIME:

25 Minutes

TOTAL TIME:

60 Minutes

SERVES:

6

INGREDIENTS

1 ready-made store bought pie crust

2 zucchini

1 yellow squash

2 tbsp olive oil

2 tsp Italian Seasoning

1 tsp basil, dried

Pinch salt (optional)

Pinch freshly ground black pepper (optional)

1 egg, beaten

2 tbsp water

DIRECTIONS

1. Preheat oven to 375 degrees.

2. Using a spiralizer or julienne peeler, spiralize the zucchini and yellow squash into spaghetti size noodles. Toss with olive oil, Italian seasoning, basil, and salt and pepper, if using. Let squash marinate for 30 minutes.

3. Prepare the pie crust according to package directions.

4. Drain squash. Roll squash noodles around each other into a circular ring. When the ring gets to 1 1/2 inches smaller in diameter than the pie crust, place it in the middle of the crust. Gently fold the 1 1/2 rim of pie dough over the squash and fold and desired.

5. Whisk the egg and water together. Brush egg mixture on pastry edges.

6. Bake for 20 to 25 minutes, or until the squash is tender and top is crispy.

7. Cool on a wire rack before serving.

Sweet and Savory Vegetarian and Gluten-free Kugel

PREP TIME:

5 Minutes

COOK TIME:

65 Minutes

TOTAL TIME:

70 Minutes

SERVES:

8

INGREDIENTS

2 tbsp butter

4 cups chopped leeks

2 1/2 lbs russet potatoes (about 7 to 8 medium)

3 eggs

2 cups ricotta cheese

3 tbsp milk

1 tbsp nutmeg

3 tbsp gluten-free flour

Kosher salt

Freshly ground black pepper

DIRECTIONS

1. Preheat oven to 400 degrees.

2. In a skillet over medium heat, sauté leeks in butter 3 to 5 minutes, or until soft. Remove leeks from pan with a slotted spoon and transfer to a plate.

3. Using a spiralizer or julienne peeler, spiralize the potatoes into spaghetti size noodles. Place in a colander to drain.

4. Whisk together eggs, ricotta cheese, milk, nutmeg, flour, salt and pepper.

5. Blend potatoes into egg mixture. Mix well. Pour potato mixture into a greased 9x11-inch baking dish. Bake 1 hour, or until golden brown and set. Allow to cool 5 minutes. Cut and serve.

Sweet Potato Pizza Pie

Inspired by the traditional Southern sweet potato pie, this sweet potato pizza with creamy cheese is a warm and comforting fall treat.

PREP TIME:

5 Minutes

COOK TIME:

15 Minutes

TOTAL TIME:

20 Minutes

SERVES:

6

INGREDIENTS

1 12-inch store-bought pizza crust

12 oz cream cheese, softened

1/2 tsp ground nutmeg

1 tbsp olive oil

5 medium sweet potatoes, spiralized

3 tbsp butter, melted

3/4 cup packed brown sugar

1/3 cup all-purpose flour

1 cup chopped pecans or walnuts

DIRECTIONS

1. Preheat oven to 425 degrees F.

2. Place pizza crust on a baking sheet. Spread cream cheese over crust. Sprinkle nutmeg over cream cheese.

3. Using a spiralizer or julienne peeler, spiralize the sweet potatoes into spaghetti size noodles. In a medium skillet, heat olive over medium heat. Add sweet potato noodles and sauté for 4 to 6 minutes, or until just soft. Remove from skillet with thongs and scatter sweet potatoes evenly over cheese.

4. Mix together melted butter, brown sugar, flour and nuts with fork. Sprinkle evenly over top of casserole.

5. Bake pizza for 10 minutes, or until hot and bubbly. Cool 3 minutes, or until cheese sets and pizza is still warm.

Delicata Squash with Rosemary, Sage and Apple Cider Glaze

Delicata squash is a mild but colorful squash that makes a delectable and eye catching side dish.

PREP TIME:

2 Minutes

COOK TIME:

25 Minutes

TOTAL TIME:

27 Minutes

SERVES:

6

INGREDIENTS

2 medium delicata squash, spiralized

3 tbsp butter

1/4 cup coarsely chopped fresh sage

1tbsp coarsely chopped fresh rosemary leaves

1 1/2 cups apple cider

1 cup water

2 tsp red wine vinegar

1/2 tsp salt

Pinch freshly ground black pepper (optional)

DIRECTIONS

1. Do not peel the skin from the delicata squash. Using a spiralizer or julienne peeler, spiralize the delicata squash into wide noodles.

2. In a large skillet, melt the butter over low heat. Add the sage and rosemary and cook 3 to 5 minutes, or until butter starts to turn golden brown.

3. Add the squash, apple cider, water, vinegar and salt. Simmer over medium heat, stirring occasionally,15 to 20 minutes or until the cider has boiled down to a glaze and the squash is tender. Season with salt and pepper, if using.

Roasted Squash Focaccia

A quick and easy version of focaccia that will delight your senses with the crispy, sweetness of squash and the intriguing flavors of herbs.

PREP TIME:

5 Minutes

COOK TIME:

45 Minutes

TOTAL TIME:

50 Minutes

SERVES:

6

INGREDIENTS

5 tbsp olive oil, divided + more for brushing

1 lb whole wheat pizza dough

1 butternut squash (about 1 1/2 lbs)

Kosher salt

Freshly cracked pepper

1 tsp chopped fresh rosemary

Honey

2 tsp thyme leaves

1/4 tsp coarse sea salt

DIRECTIONS

1. Preheat the oven to 400°F.

2. Add 3 tbsp oil into a 9-inch-round cake pan and tilt to coat. Place dough into the pan and use your hands to gently stretch dough. Flip dough over so both sides are coated with oil. Stretch dough until it evenly covers the bottom of the pan.

3. Using a spiralizer or julienne peeler, spiralize the butternut squash into wide noodles. In a large bowl, toss 2 tbsp olive oil, kosher salt and pepper with the squash noodles. Spread the slices on 1 to 2 baking sheets and roast for 15 minutes, or until tender. Remove from oven and let cool completely.

4. Increase oven temperature to 450°F.

4. Press the cooled butter nut squash into the pizza dough, curling the squash as you go. Sprinkle with rosemary. Brush the focaccia with olive oil. Bake 25 to 30 minutes, or until risen and brown on top. Cool bread on a wire rack for 5 minutes. Drizzle lightly with honey and sprinkle with thyme and sea salt. Serve warm.

Chapter 4
Dressings and Sauces

Versatile Meat Sauce

Creamy Tomato Sauce

Classic Vinaigrette

Basil-Garlic Dressing

Lemon-Chive Dressing

Peanut Lime Dressing

Creamy Avocado Sauce

Versatile Meat Sauce

This hearty meat sauce does not contain tomatoes which make it so easy to use in a variety of dishes.

PREP TIME:

10 Minutes

COOK TIME:

25 Minutes

TOTAL TIME:

35 Minutes

MAKES:

4 cups

INGREDIENTS

3 pieces bacon, chopped

2 tbsp olive oil

2 cups diced carrots

2 cups diced beets

1 cup chopped onion

1 celery stalk, chopped

5 garlic cloves, minced

2 tsp salt

1/4 tsp ground black pepper

3/4 cup dry red wine or red wine vinegar

1 cup chicken stock

2 bay leaves

1 tbsp fresh basil, chopped

1 1/2 tsp dried oregano

1/2 tsp dried thyme

1 tbsp apple cider vinegar

1 pound ground beef

DIRECTIONS

1. In a large saucepan, cook the bacon until done. Remove bacon from pan and set aside. Add olive oil to the saucepan with the bacon drippings. Add the onions and garlic and sauté 3 to 4 minutes, or until the onions are translucent.

2. Crumble the bacon and add back to the saucepan. Add the carrots, beets, and celery and cook until the vegetables have softened slightly, about 5-6 minutes.

3. Add the wine and chicken stock. Bring to a boil. Reduce heat to medium-low and simmer for 10 minutes. Remove from heat.

4. Use an immersion blender or hand mixer to blend ingredients on low speed for 15 to 20 seconds. Increase speed and blend until smooth.

5. In a separate pan, brown the ground beef and crumble while cooking into smaller bits. Do not drain.

6. Add the ground beef, bay leaves, basil, oregano, thyme, and vinegar to the sauce. Bring to a simmer and cook over medium heat for 8 to 10 minutes, or until flavors are melded. If sauce is too thick, add chicken stock in small quantities until desired consistency is reached.

Creamy Tomato Sauce

A cool, flavorful dressing that works on many types of spiralized vegetables.

PREP TIME:

5 Minutes

COOK TIME:

0 Minutes

TOTAL TIME:

5 Minutes

SERVES:

1

INGREDIENTS

2 medium Roma tomatoes

1 garlic clove, minced

1 tsp tahini

1 1/2 tsp dried basil

1/2 tsp oregano

1/4 tsp salt

DIRECTIONS

2. Add tomatoes, garlic, tahini, basil, oregano, and salt to blender. Blend until smooth.

Classic Vinaigrette

MAKES:

1/2 cup

INGREDIENTS:

2 tbsp honey

1 tbsp red wine vinegar

3 tbsp olive oil

1 tbsp country Dijon mustard

Salt and pepper to taste

DIRECTIONS:

1. Place all of the ingredients for the dressing in a bowl and whisk together. Taste and adjust to your preference.

Basil-Garlic Dressing

MAKES:

1 cup

INGREDIENTS:

1/3 cup (75 mL) olive oil

1/4 cup (60 mL) lemon juice

1/4 cup (60 mL) loosely packed basil leaves finely chopped

1 tbsp (15 mL) honey

1 clove garlic minced

1/2 tsp (2 mL) salt

1/4 tsp (1 mL) freshly ground pepper

DIRECTIONS:

1. Dressing: Whisk olive oil with lemon juice, basil, honey, garlic, salt and pepper; set aside.

Lemon-Chive Dressing

Makes:

1/2 cup

Ingredients:

2 tbsp apple cider vinegar

1/2 large lemon juice of

Salt and pepper to taste

1 tbsp olive oil

1 tbsp freshly chopped chives

1 tsp honey

DIRECTIONS

1. Combine all ingredients for the dressing into a bowl and whisk.

Peanut Lime Dressing

MAKES:

3/4 cup

INGREDIENTS

3 cloves garlic minced (about 1 tbsp)

2 tbsp tightly packed cilantro

2 tbsp natural peanut butter

2 tbsp + 2 tsp lime juice

1 tbsp + 1/2 tsp tamari

1 tbsp rice vinegar

1 tbsp peeled and chopped ginger

2 tsp coconut milk

1 1/2 tsp organic sugar

3/4 tsp sesame oil

3/4 tsp sambal oelek

1/2 cup sunflower oil

DIRECTIONS

1. In a blender, puree all ingredients except the sunflower oil.

2. With blender running, add sunflower oil in a thin stream until dressing is smooth.

Creamy Avocado Sauce

A zesty creamy sauce that is delicious on top of vegetable noodles, especially zucchini noodles.

MAKES:

1/2 cup

INGREDIENTS

2 avocados

1/2 lemon juiced

2 garlic cloves, minced

1 tbsp olive oil

Pinch salt

Pinch freshly ground black pepper

DIRECTIONS

1. In a large bowl, add avocados, lemon juice, garlic, remaining olive oil and salt and pepper. Mash with a fork until a creamy yet chunky consistency is reached.

COOK'S NOTE:

Sauce can be made ahead and refrigerated in a tightly sealed container for up to 3 days.

Soy Ginger Sauce

This delightful Asian inspired sauce is an excellent dipping sauce for veggies and also adds a nice touch to salads and wraps.

MAKES:

1 cup

INGREDIENTS

1/2 cup low-sodium soy sauce

1/4 cup rice wine vinegar

2 tablespoons fincly grated ginger

2 tablespoons chopped green onion

2 medium cloves garlic, minced

2 teaspoons sugar

1 teaspoon sesame oil

DIRECTIONS

1. Put all of the ingredients in a bowl and mix well.

From the Author

I cannot thank you enough for your interest in my Spiralizer Cookbook. I sincerely hope you have found recipes that you love and will keep at your favorites. Even more, I hope I have inspired you to use more vegetables in your cooking and find whichever spiral vegetable cutter you have chosen to be a valuable addition to your kitchen.

I would love to hear from you. If you have a moment, like what the recipes you've tried and would recommend these to others, please write a review on Amazon or visit me at www.foodthymes.com for more recipes and inspiration.

I know reviews do take time, so if you'd just like to get more recipes and learn more about how I believe strongly that food, cooking and meals are what binds us and brings more favorable memories than just about anything else, join me at www.foodthymes.com

Check out more of my #1 Best Selling Cookbooks

150 Best Breakfast Sandwich Maker Recipes
http://amzn.to/1xxtu8q

Jams and Jellies: Preserving By The Pint In Minutes: Delicious Fresh Preserves You Can Make In Under 30 Minutes With A Jam and Jelly Maker

http://amzn.to/1sK9hbr

I appreciate you being my customer!

Thank you, Jennifer